Praise for *The Tao of the Side Hustle*

"The 'qi' (energy) of Don Hyun Kiolbassa captures the intersection of ancient core values and the ever-changing circumstances of today's world. His success is the reward of diligence, sincerity, and gratitude. His lessons are applicable for everyone who wants to live mindfully with purpose."

—Dr. Karen Eng, Chair, Board of Directors, National Asian/Pacific Islander American Chamber of Commerce and Entrepreneurship

"Donald Hyun Kiolbassa reminds me of a character that climbs into a phone booth dressed as a successful young lawyer only to emerge as a trained ninja. The alchemy of his skills are spun into gold in this riveting book that shows you how to use Buddhist principles to achieve success in the business world."

—Peter J. Birnbaum, Chief Justice, Illinois Court of Claims, and CEO, Attorneys' Title Guaranty Fund Inc.

"Don Hyun Kiolbassa has knowledge and skills to help small businesses grow and protect their wealth and now he is sharing his insights and experiences from multiple startups with the business world."

—George Mui, Founder, Asian American Executive Network (formerly with the US Department of Commerce and White House Initiative on Asian Americans and Pacific Islanders)

"Don Hyun Kiolbassa's multiple side hustles and business ventures are all based on the ideas in this book. We know these lessons will work because Don's businesses are living proof. Don and this book are the real deal."

—John O'Brien, J.D., president of IRELA (Illinois Real Estate Lawyer Association) and former President of the ISBA (Illinois State Bar)

"By adapting the wisdom of Chinese Martial Arts to the modern era, Don has adapted timeless wisdom to a practical path for people to follow to a more resilient financial future."

—Jon Cesaretti, Principal, Public Accounting

THE TAO
OF THE
SIDE
HUSTLE

THE TAO
OF THE
SIDE
HUSTLE

A Buddhist Martial Arts
Approach to
Your New Business

DON HYUN KIOLBASSA

Matt Holt Books
An Imprint of BenBella Books, Inc.
Dallas, TX

Matt Holt is an imprint of BenBella Books, Inc.
10440 N. Central Expressway
Suite 800
Dallas, TX 75231
benbellabooks.com
Send feedback to feedback@benbellabooks.com

BenBella and *Matt Holt* are federally registered trademarks.

Printed in the United States of America
10 9 8 7 6 5 4 3 2 1

Library of Congress Control Number: 2022019216
ISBN 9781637741962 (hardcover)
ISBN 9781637741979 (electronic)

Editing by Katie Dickman
Copyediting by Jennifer Greenstein
Proofreading by Leah Baxter and Jenny Rosen
Text design and composition by PerfecType, Nashville, TN
Cover design by Brigid Pearson
Cover photo by Brian McConkey
Cover image © Shutterstock / cl2004lhy (Wu character)
Printed by Lake Book Manufacturing

*To my wife, Emily Holmes, and my two daughters, Ellie
Kai and Victoria Hyun. You are my motivation.*

CONTENTS

PART 3 | **SCALE**

INTRODUCTION

FOR NEARLY 250 YEARS, SINCE ADAM SMITH PUBLISHED *THE Wealth of Nations*, economics has taught that money is generally earned in three ways: through employment, entrepreneurship, and investing. Employment leads to a salary. Entrepreneurship leads to profit. Investing leads to appreciation and passive income.

The purpose of this book is to guide you from employment to entrepreneurship, or from salary to profit.

Why is it so important that you move from salary to profit? For many people out there, keeping up with the cost of living is getting harder and harder.

The American Dream of going to college, getting a job, buying a house, and having a family looks a lot different today than it did seventy years ago.

Today, to go to school, you take out debt.

You get a job, but you may hate the job *and* not make enough to get ahead.

You buy a house, you take out more debt.

You have a family, your expenses balloon to unsustainable levels.

Your parents may have been able to buy a house, take vacations, and save for retirement. For example, my father bought his house in Chicago in the 1970s for $55,000, at a time when one year of college tuition was $1,000. Good luck trying to get that today.

1

Many of us have the same American Dream as our parents did. We want to go to college, buy a house, and have a family. But for too many of us, these now feel like unattainable luxuries. Today's cost of living is *nuts*, and unfortunately, it is probably not going to get any better.

However, there is hope. There is a modern approach to achieving the American Dream available to all of us—the side hustle. A side hustle is great for two reasons.

First, if you do it right, it can help you make ends meet and get ahead—either while you have a job or when your job fails you. Second, it can act as an incubator to test out your ideas until you find one that works for you.

It's no exaggeration to say that entrepreneurship through side hustles saved my life. No, I did not make billions creating some revolutionary tech company. Those cases are highly publicized, but they are extremely rare.

Instead, I did something much more manageable. Something that anyone reading this book can do. I was broke and I hated my job. And then I started several side hustles, and one of them became successful enough to mature into a successful family business. That business gave me control over my life and brought me happiness.

While living in China, I learned that the word *Tao* loosely translates to "the Way." In this book, I want to show you the way to regain financial control over your life and bring more happiness into it.

The title of this book refers to Tao, while the subtitle refers to Buddhism. These are two different schools of thought. I use both terms intentionally, and I want to explain why.

I studied with some of the martial artists of Wudang Mountain in Shiyan, China, who generally follow Taoism, which teaches that all creatures should live in balance with the earth.

At Wudang Mountain we would sneak away to train in baguazhang. Bagua is an internal martial art, which loosely translates to "eight palms." When the Wudang martial artists train in bagua, their main-anchor basic training is a movement called "mud walking." Mud walking is moving forward in what appears to be circular movements, but the walkers are actually making the symbol of the octagon on the floor.

This is important, because the symbol for Tao, called a bagua, is an octagon with a yin and yang in the middle.

These martial artists take the word *Tao* so seriously that they literally walk in such a way as to replicate the symbol of Tao on the ground. (This gives the phrase "talking the talk, walking the walk" a whole new meaning.)

Taoism is practiced at Wudang Mountain. But I met my Wudang Mountain kung fu brothers at the Shaolin Temple in Dengfeng, China, where I trained. The Shaolin Temple is considered by many to be the birthplace of Buddhism.

The monks of the Shaolin Temple taught through stories, and following that tradition, you'll find a story in each chapter of this book.

Thus, what follows includes Taoist and Buddhist concepts from both legendary places, Wudang Mountain and the Shaolin Temple. Taoism and Buddhism are not the same thing, but I hope you'll get a lot of value from both.

We will walk a similar path through side hustles with the same dedication as these martial artists. Side hustles will become our "Tao." No need to learn to bagua mud walk.

How did I get into side hustles? Well, I had no choice. I was forced into it.

My story began like that of many others. I was super hardworking and wanted to make a difference in the world. I never really lived beyond my means, and I had very basic expectations. I did not really want an expensive car, a huge mansion, or anything luxurious. I just wanted to be in a solid financial situation.

In college, I worked some rough jobs to make ends meet, such as waiting tables at a sushi restaurant, cleaning restaurant refrigerators (I can still smell that moldy old food), scrubbing rust off used metal shelving for resale, stocking shelves, and delivering food.

Even then, I was looking beyond the long hours and hard work of a regular job, so I began a series of side hustles—some good and some bad. I started a series of small businesses. From deejaying parties, to running a promotional company, to operating a security company, to teaching martial arts to kids, these side hustles were a brutal grind, but believe it or not, I made some money from them.

I eventually stopped the side hustle life. I did what everyone told me to do. I went to college and majored in accounting. I didn't love it—actually, I never even really liked it. But the counselors at the Career Services office at my college said there was a great chance of getting a job in accounting after graduation, so I went with it. I mean, everyone needs an accountant, right?

Well, yes—except I graduated from college in Chicago in 2001, just as the collapse of Enron destroyed the biggest Chicago-based accounting firm, Arthur Anderson, and with it, any hopes I had of getting a job in accounting. I had just spent four years of my life and all this money for a degree that could not land me a job.

I tried to build a side hustle doing tax returns. At first it looked promising. I was able to convince my friends and family to let me handle filing their basic tax returns. However, I was soon crushed: low-cost do-it-yourself tax preparation software products launched at almost that exact same time. They offered to do the same tax returns I was doing for $19.99. I could not compete. I'd gone to college, worked hard, chosen a "safe" direction—and I couldn't make a living.

When I went back to Career Services, guess what the counselors told me? That the job market is competitive. That in order to compete, what I really should do is come back to school for more education. Then they recommended law school.

And like the good little worker bee that I was, I believed them.

Part of what I believed was the data law schools were presenting, about graduation rates and job placements. Turns out, these data were . . . let's just say, subject to interpretation—for example, the law schools counted recent grads as employed whether they had full-time jobs with law firms or part-time jobs as baristas. And they counted only the grads who bothered to respond to the survey, which few of the unemployed had the time or interest to do.

And law school tuition was insanely expensive. I couldn't remotely afford it. "Take out some loans," the admissions officers told me. "See how much our graduates make."

Getting a loan was easy. I just filled out a government form or two, sent them in, and before long, I was in a massive amount of debt.

After three years of law school and more than $200,000 in student loans from law school and undergrad, I graduated into an even worse job market. The 2008 financial crisis hit and destroyed the economy worldwide. Every day brought news of more big companies going out of business. Every kind of business shed jobs. Hiring froze.

There were no jobs available. None.

I lived on credit cards, adding to the credit card debt I'd already started building as a student. Months later, I finally landed a paying job doing tax returns at a law firm. Not as a lawyer, which I'd just spent the last three years training to be, but as a support staffer doing low-level accounting work.

I was making $42,500 in annual salary, with $220,000 in student loans and rising credit card debt. That worked out to about $3,000 a month in after-tax take-home pay, with about $1,800 set aside per month for student loan payments. It didn't take long for me to realize this was not okay.

Man, I shudder just thinking about it.

I had to live on $1,200 per month. My expenses exceeded my income by so much, but there was no way for me to cut back any further—I mean, there's just no way around paying rent and buying food.

I clearly remember having to borrow money from my father for the train. Here I was—Mr. Big Shot College Degree, Mr. Accountant, Mr. Law Degree—borrowing money just to pay for my commute to work.

And to make matters worse? The job was terrible. My bosses tortured me. On my first day, I overheard my boss call me "cheap labor." There was no room for growth. Heck, they treated me like I was lucky just to have this terrible job.

I was miserable.

I looked into filing bankruptcy. But bankruptcy would not get rid of my student loans. I was trapped in a financial cage of my own making.

This misery poured into my personal life. All my friendships and relationships fell apart because I was so awful to be around. My closest friends hated being around me. I would always talk about how horrible the world was to me. I was the kind of guy the self-help books tell you to stay away from.

Dating? Forget about it. Who wants to date someone who is a complete financial train wreck? Even if someone did want to go out on a date, I was too broke to pay. All I could think about was the conversation we'd have to have if things worked out. "Oh, by the way, I need you to cosign my enormous loan." Nobody wants that. Think of my online dating profile: "Dead broke, can't even file for bankruptcy." Not many swipes right for that one.

I clearly remember the single lowest moment of my life. I was lying on an inflatable mattress in my father's unfinished attic. I'd finally had enough. I went completely numb. For twenty-eight years of my life, I had never stopped doing what everyone told me to do, and yet nothing had worked. And I was sick of it. I just stopped caring.

I am really embarrassed to admit this, but I thought about ending it all. I just knew that I could not live this way forever.

But . . . as I lay there, steeping in my own misery, I tried to remember the last time I'd been happy. And I had a flashback. I realized that the last time I had been truly happy was when I trained in martial arts.

Now, let me back up a moment. My father is American and my mother is from South Korea. They met in Korea, and while she came to this country with him as a young bride, my father raised me. He thought getting me involved with martial arts would be a great way to connect me to my Asian heritage.

So I have been involved in different forms of martial arts and combat sports since I was four years old. Growing up, I trained under a few coaches in the United States. But in the summers, I was sent to Korea, China, and South America to train. This gave me a broad perspective on life and martial arts.

Humbly speaking, I would say I was considered pretty decent in my chosen sport. When I was younger, I was in all kinds of martial arts magazines. I won tournaments all over the world. I appeared in DVDs featuring my techniques. I was a gold medalist for the United States Wushu

Team. That led to an invitation no other Westerner had received: to live and train as a monk at the Shaolin Temple in China.

But that day in my father's attic, lying on an air mattress, all that success seemed long ago and far away. I was so miserable, but I realized that I had once been happy. And so I decided that I would look up one of my old coaches to see if I could train with her.

She had coached me in wushu, which literally translates to "Chinese war arts." Actually, the whole name is wushu kung fu—but the "kung fu" part just translates to "practice."

She suggested that we work out together. And when we did . . . well, for a moment I felt alive again.

I mentioned to her that I was having a bumpy time. Actually, it was all I could do to keep myself from vomiting up all my problems to her.

She said something I'll never forget: "Don, get back to your training basics. Your basics develop your instincts. In life and fighting, you have to rely on your instincts."

It dawned on me that I had stopped listening to my instincts. For example, I had stopped doing the side hustles that were actually making me money, and I was listening to all these people telling me to do something that was not working and that I hated.

My family used to say that your instincts are your ancestors trying to guide you. Maybe that is part of it, but I think it is you trying to survive. Since the beginning of time, we as humans have survived on our instincts. Somewhere along the way, I had stopped listening to my own.

I began training with my old coach. Soon after, someone took a video of me working out at a gym, doing a relatively rare form of martial arts. He posted that video online, which got the attention of an old friend, who . . . well, one thing led to another, and I was asked to film the motion capture for a major project for a big studio. Motion capture is a process in which you wear a special suit with markers that allows cameras to track your movements. Once the movement is recorded, animators are able to put their art over the movements to make their animated characters move like the motion capture model.

I was offered the opportunity to demonstrate my martial arts in a major video game. I had a very small part filming the intro for the release. I was so nervous, because I had no acting or film experience.

But I was so excited that I was willing to do some of the craziest stunts and moves, wearing this super-tight Velcro suit with cameras catching my every move. I actually walked out with several injuries, but I did not want to disclose this to anyone for fear of getting cut. I did stuff that I swear would break my bones today, but I gave that opportunity everything I had.

Those few days saved my life. First, they reminded me how to have fun. Second, when I got that check, I was reinvigorated. For that month, I actually got ahead a little. I decided that if my employer was not going to help me get ahead, I was going to do whatever I needed to do to make ends meet. I was going to take back control of my destiny.

I needed to side hustle.

For the next twelve years, I continued my motion capture side hustle. I filmed martial arts motion capture for some of the biggest action franchises in the industry. The rope dart? Superheroes and villains? Undead ninjas? That's me.

I did not make life-changing money—it was solid and generous, but I still had a lot of bills and debt.

What I gained was a change in mentality. All of a sudden, there was an avenue for me to succeed that was not completely dependent on my cruel employer. I wanted to take back control of my life through side hustles.

I started several other side hustles. And then one of them took off and grew into a sustainable small business.

This book is not about how cool I am, but about how amazing you are going to be. I was helped by lucky breaks—I was extremely lucky that someone filmed and posted a video of me and someone with hiring authority saw it—but this is quite frankly a rare situation. Besides this one super-cool side hustle, I have been involved in many not-so-glamorous, but exponentially more profitable, side hustles that anyone can do.

Getting out there and hustling can work for anyone.

Why should you listen to me? That is the big question. Your time is valuable, and there are a lot of books out there from much more impressive authors.

But my average abilities might be the reason you should read this book. This book is for people as normal as you and me. There's nothing about me that is particularly impressive. I got average grades, I have an average IQ, and I have an average physique.

However, I was able to make the transition from salary to profit, not because I am awesome, but because I followed a very specific set of principles.

You probably already know a little bit of Chinese war strategy— maybe without even realizing it! It's been popularized over the past decades by literally dozens of editions of Sun Tzu's famous book, *The Art of War*. But *The Art of War*, while a great read, is 2,500 years old and written for generals. Different and more practical variations of these strategic principles have been taught in wushu for generations. Variations that teach you to take slow, gradual steps toward victory.

Sun Tzu was writing for the generals, but this book is for the foot soldier, the underdog, the person trying to make it. *The Art of War* was originally written for the elite—not the full-time working parent juggling job, kids, and debt. Not the recent college grad with a mountain of student loans and no idea what to do. Not the person who followed the rules and did all the things they were supposed to do, but still can't make ends meet.

Finally, why now? It is my belief that we are about to enter a new era of technology that will create incredible opportunities for small businesses. I do not want to get too technical here, but currently technology companies are controlled by a small, very powerful group. All their power is derived from driving traffic and control of users (generally through the content of creatives), which is one of the reasons our data are so important (so they can target their marketing at us).

For example, look at the music industry. It seems crazy that the musicians who actually create the art do not have a higher level of control over their own product. Instead, the platforms that distribute the music have much of the power.

I believe the internet will become more decentralized, providing opportunities for small businesses and giving creatives more power over what they make.

This is the time to give this a shot.

PART 1

SIDE HUSTLE

TO EMBODY TAO, THE MARTIAL ARTISTS OF WUDANG MOUN-tain walk in a pattern in the shape of an octagon. Similarly, we will embody the Tao of the side hustle by walking in the following pattern. To guide us, this book is broken up into three parts:

1. **Part 1:** Chapters 1–5 outline some basics you need to start your side hustle. If business is war, you must control these five anchor assets in order to win the war. These are your fundamental basics, which you should build into your muscle memory to fall back on regardless of your business and market conditions. Whether I am talking to a side hustler, start-up founder, CEO, or CFO, I always start with these five assets.

   As in any good old-school kung fu movie, you—our hero from humble beginnings—have hit rock bottom and need to work your way up to face and fight the main villain. We begin with your training ground to work on the basics. (Insert training montage here!)

You will need these basics to enhance your instincts. Life and business move fast. These basics are universal and will help you adapt to a rapidly changing future.

2. **Part 2:** Chapters 6–10 outline steps to stabilize your side hustle. When your side hustle starts working, you will need to stabilize it. This is the part of the movie where you have built up some skill and are ready to fight the small bad guys. You may try several side hustles until you find one that is capable of growing. If you have one hundred side hustles, you do not need one hundred success stories. You just need one of them to work.

3. **Part 3:** Chapters 11–15 contain highly technical content. This is where we discuss ways to scale up your side hustle to a small or midsize business. This is the part of the movie where you are ready to face and fight the main bad guy and become the hero of the story. If your side hustle matures into a small business, you may want to scale up your operation. These chapters are reserved for the side hustles that have materialized and are functional.

So we'll start with some basics on the training ground and gradually work our way into advanced techniques. It may be time for you to turn your back on the crowd and follow your instincts.

> For all you foot soldiers out there not born with a silver spoon in your mouth, your Tao is the side hustle. This is your "Way."

Let's start walking.

CHAPTER 1 ☯ SKILLS

*The first step of the Tao of the side
hustle is to develop a skill.*

TO JOIN A POKER TABLE, YOU NEED TO ANTE UP. YOU MUST
have value to offer.

If you come from humble beginnings like me, determining your
skills is your first step. If you do not have obvious assets to offer, you
must become the asset. The best way to become an asset is to develop a
necessary skill.

In martial arts, in order to stand on the battlefield, you must have
some skill. Whether you are a general, an archer, or a cavalry soldier, your
skill gets you to the table. Your skill is your ante.

The same is true of starting a side hustle. But where do you begin?
How do you go about finding your ante?

A young monk once approached an elder monk and asked, "Will you
be my guru and teach me to be the best I can be?"

15

The old monk chuckled at the request but respected the young monk for asking. The old monk said, "Yes, of course I can teach you. But you must first help me feed the animals." The young monk immediately agreed, and the two walked toward the animals.

The old monk approached the first animal, a tiger. The monk kept the tiger in a secluded pit to prevent it from attacking the other animals.

The old monk instructed the young monk to throw some meat into the tiger pit. The old monk promised that once they were done feeding the animals, he would teach the young monk to reach his full potential. The young monk happily agreed.

The two reached the tiger pit and began feeding the tiger. The young monk was so excited that he feverishly began throwing meat over the side. The old monk took this opportunity to ask, "Now, are you sure you want me to teach you to reach your full potential?" The young monk said, "Yes, of course." The old monk smiled.

The old monk took a piece of the meat, stuck it in the belt of the *gi* the young monk was wearing, and pushed the young monk into the tiger pit.

The young monk was in a complete panic as he realized what the old man had done. The tiger immediately began to pursue the young monk. The young monk tried to climb back up the wall, but the tiger ran and cut him off. The young monk tried to climb a branch of a tree, but the tiger jumped and broke the branch. The young monk tried to run away, but the speedy tiger quickly caught up to him.

Finally, the tiger cornered the young monk. The young monk was face-to-face with the "king" and ready to face death. The tiger, salivating for the taste of meat, flexed his muscles as he approached the young boy.

The tiger leaped toward the young monk, extending a claw. The young monk jumped away with everything in his soul. The tiger slashed but could only reach the back of the young monk. The belt broke, releasing the piece of meat to the ground. The tiger jumped on the meat.

While the tiger was distracted, the young monk took his opportunity and climbed up the wall. The young monk, panting, yelled at the old monk, "Are you crazy? I almost died! I barely got out."

The old monk said, "My son, you will never know how fast you can run until a tiger chases you."

Nothing will motivate you like getting chased by a tiger. My tiger was the financial pressures of the increased cost of living.

In old-school Chinese war arts—wushu—you need to find a specialty. Centuries ago, you needed some specific weapon or skill to be on the battlefield. For example, the most skilled warriors got a straight-sword nickname, "Scholar Sword" or "Jian," and the less skilled warriors got a broadsword nickname, "Peasant Sword" or "Dao." The lowest of the low got either the wooden-staff nickname, "Goon," or the bare-hand nickname, "Quan."

I definitely would have been on the low end of the totem pole.

Discovering your skill is a journey. You should cast a wide net, and when you finally catch the idea you are looking for, it will probably grow, expand, retract, and evolve as you get older. You should start broadly with what interests you. Then, as you walk that path of interest, you need to discover something in that world that you want to focus on. When you make that discovery, narrow in on the part of that universe that interests you and become the best at it.

For example, if you were interested in martial arts that focus on striking, you would sample muay Thai, karate, tae kwon do, boxing, or sanda. You'd get to know these arts and pick one to specialize in.

I experienced many different martial arts styles and teachers. I decided to focus on wushu because I love the depth of the style. I decided to become completely dominant in one skill.

I chose *shen biao* (rope dart/dagger) because I really had fun practicing it and audiences loved it. When I was bored, I would pick it up to play. Over time I became extremely good at this small sliver of the wushu universe.

The only reason I was given the opportunity to film motion capture for big film and game projects is that I had become dominant in a specific skill set. Humbly and respectfully, I am one of the best *shen biao* practitioners in the world.

I am solid in other things, but I am absolutely dominant in that skill.

As I left my martial arts life and phased into my professional life, I forgot this principle of being dominant in one skill. I had teachers and counselors tell me to turn my weaknesses into my strengths. I do not like this advice at all. If you follow it, you become a generalist who is not dominant at anything.

I began my law career trying out family law, tax law, and criminal law. Then I sampled property law, and it really interested me. I found it fun and even studied it during my free time. It was not a chore to me. Slowly I became dominant at small parts of the area of property law.

See how I sampled a wide variety of areas, then hyperfocused when I found something that interested me? Find an area that interests you, then experience it by sampling the things on the menu. Find that thing in the universe that really motivates you. Be hyperspecific in your choice. Think in terms of your enjoyment and the needs of your universe. You have to know yourself and be honest with yourself.

> You do not have to be amazing at everything. Pick something in the universe that you really enjoy and run with it. Do not try to turn your weaknesses into strengths. Become dominant at a specific skill that is in alignment with your strengths. The universe will then always need you. You are now in demand.

You may be thinking, "Don, you graduated with debt, sure—but you came out with a CPA and a JD. I do not have a skill set like that."

It's true, *but degrees aren't skills.*

Law school teaches you to think like a lawyer, but not how to do anything practical. There is no apprenticeship, no residency program. You start your legal career knowing legal principles and literally nothing about how to actually be a lawyer.

In other words, I had fancy diplomas on my wall but no real skills, and a huge debt to repay. I literally did not know how to *do* anything.

> **You need to have a value—a reason for being on the battlefield.**

I generally knew that I enjoyed property law. I always wanted to own stuff, and I wanted to know the rules around that ownership. I wanted to help other people learn as well, but it was clear that I didn't yet have the skills or experience to do this. So I assessed my position and made some decisions.

First, I decided to start learning. A lot. I became a learning machine. You will need to experience and relentlessly learn about the things in your universe.

Sometimes learning is not that easy. You cannot allow this to stop you. Once I discovered I really liked property law, I soon found out that no one would teach me. I could not get a job in the field or even a mentorship.

I started reaching out to my close family and friends in my network, offering to work for free—I did anything from basic contract work to document review during my lunch breaks. I knew I couldn't quit my job—I needed the money too much—but I used my lunch breaks and time after work to take on the tasks that friends and family threw my way.

(Your friends and family are the best place to start, by the way. They'll always be supportive of you and won't scrutinize you too closely if you screw up. Strangers will destroy your reputation online in an instant through online review platforms. Better to learn with people who know you and like you.)

I wasn't picky. I took on anything that came through the door. I recall some of the big-shot lawyers referring to me as "cheap Asian labor" or a "dishwasher" for doing this super-low-level work. Yeah, it was kind of humiliating, but you know what got me through everything? I was really interested in the subject area.

I had no ego. Whatever the issue was, I would spend every free minute reading and learning.

Just as with martial arts, I became obsessed with improving my skill. I spent every free moment of my life learning and practicing. I was like a ronin (a masterless samurai) to the extent that I had no teacher. No one would show me the way, so I read anything and everything I could get my hands on, looking for an angle to attack.

This wasn't glamorous. And it wasn't very profitable, especially not relative to all the debt hanging over my head. I was grinding like crazy— with no dating life and little free time, just work and exercise.

PURPOSE

Once I had discovered something that generally interested me, I needed to find my reason for existence in this universe of property law.

I thought the most important question I needed to start asking was, What is my purpose?

I realized that to get to the answer, I actually needed to ask, What problem can I solve that needs solving?

The answer to this question is often your purpose. The Shaolin monks believe that the meaning of life is to find one's purpose—a reason for being here. I learned my purpose by listening to my customers.

I started to attack low-hanging fruit in tangentially related businesses because I was not ready for high-level direct engagement in property law. By training myself in related work, I would start learning basic documents, which would teach me property law by sheer overlap.

I started to fill out documents for people pro bono. For example, most experienced lawyers do not want to touch filling out power of attorney forms. They are boilerplate forms that are tedious to update. However, almost everyone needs them. I started doing them for free for friends and family. As I was doing this work, I was able to see how these forms connected to people's property needs.

Doing pro bono power of attorney forms is the lawyer equivalent of digging trenches. It is mind-numbing work. But I learned something special while doing this. When you are digging trenches, you become friends with the people you are digging trenches with.

Doing this work helped me build friendships and relationships with some people, and a few asked me to handle their real estate closings. My customers began telling me their pain points.

> Epictetus said, "You have two ears and one mouth, so you can listen twice as much as you can speak."

My customers told me what they needed from me, and I worked toward delivering that need better than others. I had no idea what I was doing at first, but I would learn tips from clerks, closers, realtors, and title companies.

Real estate closings are a low-margin, high-punishment business. They are like carrying concrete up a building stairwell. But this work gave me additional experience and insight. Buying a home with a client is an incredibly intimate process.

Many American families hold the majority of their wealth in real estate, small businesses, and retirement plans. Through real estate closings,

I slowly began learning the ways these three worked together in a family's life. (This is the part of the movie where the hero's knuckles are bleeding from repeatedly punching the wooden dummy.)

I continued to do all this on my lunch break. The second my lunch break began, I would literally run several blocks over to title companies to crank through closings. I always begged everyone to schedule at noon. It was pretty funny—I told everyone that I was completely booked and could only do noon. Which was not technically a lie. I mean, I was working the other hours.

I was getting paid for these closings, but not a lot. I was hustling so hard, learning the checklists at night and doing the work at lunch. This is the reason that, to this day, I like to pack *kimbap* (rice and vegetables wrapped in seaweed—a Korean treat that's great for side hustlers) or hard-boiled eggs in my pocket. That is how I ate.

In my first year, I made about $4,000 from my side hustle. It was not exactly what I was hoping for financially, but things started happening during my grind.

There was no immediate gratification, but I was investing in long-term relationships with people. This built up a powerful asset: trust. People started to trust me, because they saw how serious and sincere I was. I was willing to do anything to get into the game. Clients started to recognize that attitude.

I mean, what would you as a consumer rather have, an Ivy League–educated lawyer who does not care about you or a basic solid person who is going to do anything to help you accomplish your goals? The best person is not always the right person.

Rarely does life work in straight lines. You may say to yourself that you do not want your customers creating your purpose in life. But your first side hustle is not the endgame—it is just your starting point.

Please keep in mind that your side hustle purpose does not define who you are. Your side hustle is a vehicle that should help you along your journey to reach your life purpose.

Your purpose will evolve.

You can see how I started in one area but evolved into something completely different. The same may happen to you. When you are starting, ask yourself where you can solve a problem in your chosen universe in the relatively near future.

You have to be patient in seeking opportunities. The Shaolin monks taught me patience. In a world of instant gratification, patience is a virtue lost on many. As the only loudmouthed Westerner in the group, I stuck out like a sore thumb. But they did something interesting that I appreciated later in life. Before they would allow me to enter to train with the Lohan (the most elite teachers there), I needed to kneel in front of the temple, knock, and wait for them to let me in.

So in my Western, instant-gratification, "give it to me now" mindset, waiting on my knees on concrete steps in the rain was not something I liked. But it taught me to really appreciate what the monks eventually gave me.

> Sometimes you need to sit at the door in the rain to learn something worth learning.

You find your purpose by talking to the customers in the universe you are interested in.

Now that I had a side hustle, I needed to make it my own by creating my interpretation of the solution to the problem—my style.

STYLE

After you understand your universe and identify your purpose, you should turn your attention to creating your own spin on solving the problem. In martial arts, I trained with coaches from many different backgrounds. They influenced me and gave me a broad range of perspectives.

I accumulated those perspectives and developed what I liked and what I didn't. This is how I created my style.

When I teach my students martial arts, I tell them, "Learn from my techniques, but once you master them, interpret them in your own way." This is why we say "martial *art*" instead of "fighting." It is your art. The same applies in business.

Once you get your feet underneath you, you will develop your style. From everything you learned, formulate the Tao (Path)—the way *you* want to solve the problem.

In martial arts, once you choose a weapon, you have to apply your own flavor to it. When we wield a sword, we all have the same general moves, but our differences—where we are bigger or smaller, faster or slower, and stronger or weaker—influence our strategies. We need to play to our strengths and find our own style to move with the sword.

The sword is a tool. The way you use it is your own interpretation.

The style you choose is your approach. It's exactly the same in business.

If you are fortunate enough to find an area that interests you, and then find a problem to solve that has demand and matches your abilities, you need to train yourself to solve that problem. Hopefully, you will have a mentor or coach training you, but if not, you can do as I did and become self-taught.

I did not have a lawyer mentor or coach at first. My first coach was my most important coach: my customers. I allowed them to coach me on how they wanted me to solve their problems and meet their needs. This gave me incredible perspective as I learned the most important character trait of business: empathy.

I learned all the pain points of my customers and all the places of friction and turbulence along the path toward execution. This perspective helped mold my style.

We are all walking aggregates of our past experiences. Our experiences create our perspectives. Use your perspective to interpret the best way to solve problems.

For example, look at this book. It is my interpretation of how to solve a problem.

Specifically, I am trying to provide a step-by-step guide to starting a side hustle for people with humble beginnings. This book is not for people with Ivy League business school backgrounds, because I do not have that perspective.

> Show the world *your* style of kung fu, or
> "practice," and there will be those who are
> attracted to the way *you* solve the problem.
> (There will also be people who do not like your
> approach. That is okay.)

Not everyone is going to like you or your perspective on solving a problem. Not every potential customer or client is going to be aligned with you or your approach.

That is okay. You just need to reach and attract those who do.

How do you determine your style? Measure your strengths and weaknesses relative to your terrain.

1. Strengths and Weaknesses

You must be honest with yourself and understand your strengths and weaknesses. I do not believe in turning your weaknesses into your strengths. I believe in positioning yourself to amplify your strengths and minimize your weaknesses. Your strengths will help you build, and you can make sure your weaknesses do not destroy you.

Make your strengths so dominant that they cannot be ignored. Your strengths should be able to run a train through your competition in a corresponding category. Pick a lane with the intention of dominating it.

You need to apply your strengths and weaknesses to the environment you are in. For example, if you are a great storyteller, this probably will not help you in a basketball slam dunk contest. You need to make sure that your strengths have some relevance to the environment you are working in.

2. Terrain

After you know your strengths and weaknesses, you need to understand the terrain of the ground you must cover to make sure the vehicle you create is right for the job.

This is important, so let's say it again. You have to understand the terrain of the ground you must cover to make sure the vehicle you create is right for the job.

What do I mean by *terrain*?

Think about it this way. If you need to cross an ocean to get from point A to point B, the environment is a very wide, very deep, very wet ocean. Therefore, you know you need a boat. Certain seasons are rougher than others, with calm seas during some months and rough winds and dangerous waves at other times. Therefore, you know you should set sail at a certain time. And the winds blow in a certain direction, changing hour by hour. Therefore, you know you must position your boat on the course that allows your sails to fill, and remain filled, to speed you along to your destination.

Your side hustle, your business, is just a vehicle to help you accomplish your goals. For now, your goal is getting from point A to point B—escaping from whatever is making you feel trapped and arriving at freedom, however you personally define that.

Timing is an important consideration of terrain.

Timing is everything. You don't want to have a snow-shoveling business in July.

Remember when you were in fifth grade and your science teacher taught you the scientific method? Discovering your skill/style can be approached in much the same way.

- **Research:** Go out and meet the people. Your people. What problem can you solve, and how?
- **Hypothesis:** Come up with your approach that solves a specific problem for your people.
- **Test:** Try it out.
- **Analyze:** Does it work, as measured by customer happiness?
- **Adjust:** How can you make it better?

Keep doing this over and over and over, until you get it right!

I had an anchor martial arts instructor who coached me since I was young. She taught me the concept of *shoshin*. *Shoshin* is a Japanese word that translates to "beginner's mind." This means that you need to be in a constant state of learning; you let go of your ego and everything you learned up until then.

One of the greatest lessons she taught me was to go out and learn techniques from multiple instructors.

There are two types of knowledge: substantive and procedural. We can all learn substantive knowledge from books, videos, podcasts, and online research. However, procedural knowledge is learned from experience.

The most efficient and effective way of learning procedural knowledge is to go straight to the source and find guides.

I started building up an inventory of guides—recently retired lawyers—who gave me a huge arsenal of tools and weapons. I would learn more from them in a few months than I could from working at a firm for a few years. There's just something about learning from people in the twilight of their lives—when they like you, they want to pass on their knowledge to you with an extreme sense of urgency. It is a way for them to live on.

They taught me about the business. I learned about the conditions, such as timing and cycles. I learned about controlling positions, like high ground, low ground, upstream, and downstream. I learned about combat with opponents, such as attacks, combinations, and defense. I learned about politics, including dealing with regulations, allies, and enemies. I learned the substance and procedure of the law.

I was now armed with hundreds of years of experience from people who had dedicated their lives to the trade. I felt ready to build.

In the next chapter, we discuss what to do with your skill once you've chosen one and learned it.

PRACTICE TIP

Pick a Skill

"Skills" is the longest chapter of this book because the journey to discover your first skill is usually the most difficult and most time-consuming.

Many of my friends tell me that my story is different from that of most Americans, as my background in law and martial arts is unique. While this statement may be technically true, I submit to you that virtually every one of my successful small business clients from a wide range of fields has a very similar blueprint.

Actually, I challenge the reader to look back at some of the most successful entrepreneurs today (excluding those who inherited their wealth). Every one of them followed this blueprint. Here is a quick and dirty approach.

These entrepreneurs did the following, in this order:

Step 1: Most of these entrepreneurs started in a general direction that interested them. You have to get involved in the universe you are interested in. Find problems in that universe that demand to be solved.

Step 2: These entrepreneurs found a small segment of that universe where they identified an opportunity (a need or future need) and then became hyperfocused. Once you've identified yours, you must work to master it. Over time, you will differentiate yourself by putting your own spin on the solution.

Step 3: Once the entrepreneurs stabilized their businesses, the businesses grew and evolved into greater opportunities.

This is your call to action. This blueprint works. This three-step approach will help you.

For example, let's say you have a full-time job you hate. You generally like computer science, but you are not sure what to do with that. As you get into it, you realize you want to build the next multimillion-dollar app. But you do not have the money or programming chops to pull it off.

Well, perhaps you know just enough to put together basic websites. Start by grinding away at websites for your family and friends, and gradually work your way up to more complex sites, using the money you are paid to hire someone better than you to do the parts you don't yet know and then show you how to do it. Always trade money for skill or time.

Over time, your skills will improve, you will build your network, and you will be able to take time to think of new ideas for your app when you are finally ready to build it. For example, network with people at bigger companies for small website jobs. While talking to them, they might give you ideas for ways to improve their lives.

During your downtime, you can think of ways to provide that solution.

There may be some maintenance work for which the people at these big firms do not want to pay big website developer rates. As their trust for you builds, they will come to you with bigger opportunities. Then one day, *bam!* You mastered the very solution your customers were asking for. They move all their accounts to you, and you are now a seven-figure annual reoccurring revenue (ARR) business. An overnight success twenty years in the making.

Sound like a fairy tale?

That is a real-life side hustle success story of a client of mine who now creates super-high-end websites (like sites for Fortune 500 companies) and apps for a living. He had no idea what he was doing at first, but over time became a hugely successful website and app developer.

CHAPTER 2 ☯ ARMY

*The second step of the Tao of the side hustle is
to build your army, combining and harnessing
a community to support your new skill.*

THE NEXT STEP IS TO BUILD A COMMUNITY AROUND YOU TO support your new talent. You will need to build a community of employees, clients, and mentors for your business to grow.

The reason I title this process "army" is that you will need to mobilize each group when needed.

My motion capture side hustle opportunity reinvigorated me. This small but important opportunity showed me that I needed to get out there and hustle.

Side hustling by filming big action projects with big studios is not consistent, day-to-day work, and many people are gunning for this work. (Think about it, you get paid to pretend to be a superhero!) After my initial gig, that well went dry for some time.

About a year and a half later, the studio offered me the opportunity to return to work on a different major project. They expected this project to have all kinds of crazy action, and this time there was a budget to build a whole team.

It was another incredible opportunity. But I had no idea how I was going to provide the super-high-level deliverable I knew the studio wanted.

Then I thought back to my younger days training in martial arts. In 2008, I was asked to compete in China as a member of the United States Wushu Team. This was before my side hustle journey began. Wushu is a very popular martial art in China. Since China was hosting the Olympics, wushu made a run at becoming an Olympic sport. Unfortunately, it came up short and was not selected.

This was unfortunate for me, as I won a gold medal for the US team. Since wushu fell short in becoming an official Olympic sport, I cannot identify myself as an Olympian. The silver lining? I learned a really valuable business lesson: specialize in your strengths.

As the coaches were assembling the US team, I realized that they were picking athletes who specialized in something and completely dominated that specific category. In this way, the team played each athlete to their strengths. I looked at my teammates and realized that even if I quit my specialty and only practiced theirs, I would never catch up to them. In addition, by quitting my specialty, I would not be sharpening my saw. So I would suck at everything.

When you are competing at a very high level, you will not turn your weaknesses into strengths. You need to build a team around you, with each member focused on their own strongest category. That is how you turn weaknesses into strengths and become broadly dominant in multiple categories in business. You hire and retain people better than you. Just like my wushu team did.

So I started recruiting martial artists who were specialists in their fields to the motion capture team. They were so good that I would never be able to catch up to them.

I found out that most of the top specialists were so sought after that they had a horrible attitude when I would talk to them. I could not tell them exactly what I was working on, because of nondisclosure agreements, so they kind of blew me off when I would approach them.

I just did not have the patience for this. Keep in mind that I was still working a full-time job and recruiting specialists at martial arts studios and action studios at night. (By the way, when most of these top guys found out what I was doing years later, they regretted blowing me off. Treat the person at the bottom the same as the person at the top. Be nice to everyone; you never know who they are or what they are doing.)

Rather than settle for rejections, I started asking for each person's top apprentices. These martial artists were still amazing (and way better than me at what they did well), but they had a much better attitude.

> Years later I asked the person in charge of the motion capture project why he decided to give me the opportunity. This position was highly coveted by the top action professionals in the world. With that level of competition, I figured I did not have a chance. The person who hired me said that he found me responsible, trustworthy, and accountable and thought that I would figure the rest out. I was not the best person, but I was the right person for the job. Do not try to find the best person; you need to find the right person.

Next thing I knew, I had assembled this incredibly talented team that had great chemistry. We did some of the craziest action stuff you could imagine. There was a gymnast, karate person, jiujitsu person, and more. We were all cross-training and sharing ideas with no ego. We were flying through the air kung fu–ing each other. It was crazy and the deliverable was amazing.

The funny thing about that project is that I was probably the least talented person on the team. If you ever find yourself in a room where you are the most talented at everything, you need to get yourself in a different room. Surround yourself with high achievers; this will force you to level up your game.

But even though I was not the most talented, the customer was happy! I delivered what the customer was looking for, the way the customer wanted it, at a price where everyone won. We crushed that project, and the filming and video game were very successful. Of all the projects I have been involved with, I am most proud of that one.

When filming ended, I was sure I was going to get all kinds of opportunities to film all over the world. Guess what happened? Nothing. No one called. So once again, I needed to get back to the grind of my law side hustle.

Yet I had learned a very valuable lesson from that filming: the value of a team of specialists with good chemistry coming together to bring a deliverable to the customer. In filming, my customer was the studio and it had high demands. In my law practice, the customer was someone worried about their property. Trust me: the demands were equally high.

There was once a greedy general in China. He would raid small villages too small to defend themselves. He would hire mercenaries to do this, and they secretly hated him. They would do all the work, but he would keep all the spoils.

After he conquered a village, the greedy general would erect a statue of himself bigger than the shrines to the gods. This vanity angered the gods, and they decided to teach the general a lesson.

The gods sent him a magic ring that constantly told him how handsome, smart, and powerful he was. The ring told him that his soldiers were lazy and incompetent and that all the military success was attributable to him.

The greedy general continued to go from village to village, taking from people.

There was a small, poor farming village that was run by a young man nicknamed Xiaoda. *Xiao* means "little," and *da* means "big." The people called him this because every harvest he gave the rice that he could not carry to those around him. He kept little and gave big. *Xiaoda*.

Because the farmers of the village shared so generously in the harvest, each was invested in the land and its future.

One day the greedy general came upon Xiaoda's village. He commanded his mercenaries to attack and take the village and all the rice.

But the mercenaries quickly saw that this was no ordinary village. All the farmers were willing to die for their lands. The mercenaries, on the other hand—poorly paid outsourced labor—were not willing to risk their lives for the mere scraps the general provided.

The general wanted to understand the reason behind the farmers' mentality. He snuck in under the cover of night and discovered Xiaoda's habit of giving away the rice he could not personally eat. Xiaoda's behavior had clearly created a culture of trust, hard work, and generosity amongst the workers. The workers of the village had invested their whole lives in the village and would die before giving it up.

The mercenaries refused to attack and fled from the general and the village. The greedy general, stunned, asked the young man a question. "Why would you give away your rice? Everything that you have worked for?"

Xiaoda answered simply, "If you have two hands full of rice, you cannot pick up the steak."

The general bowed. He renounced his greedy ways, shattered the god's cursed ring, and began to farm in Xiaoda's village.

You have to be generous to your employees if you expect them to stay. The goal of many companies is to maximize profit for the shareholders or owners. This objective does not work well at the side hustle or small business level. If you want your people to stay, there must be a way for them to win. Would you rather have loyal workers willing to stand next to you or mercenaries who would run at the first sight of a storm? Do not be too greedy.

EMPLOYEES

You found a skill and learned how to do it. The next step is to teach others how to do it with and for you. Be generous with your knowledge.

Employees are a huge part of your army, and when opportunities arise you need to be able to mobilize people to execute your business plan. You do not want to sell something that you cannot deliver.

I know this is counterintuitive. You just worked super hard to find and build your skill, and now I am telling you to just give it away. Actually, I'm suggesting an action that may sound even worse: you are going to pay someone to learn from you.

Hiring your first assistant is different from the kind of hiring you'll need to do later on when you're scaling your successful business. I'll talk about that hiring process later on in this book.

For now, I want to focus on hiring your first employee.

First, let me acknowledge something: at this point, you're not supporting yourself yet with your side hustle. So where do I get off suggesting that you pocket even less and share your revenue with an employee?

That was exactly what happened when I hired my first assistant. I was taking money that would normally go into my pocket and putting it into the pocket of someone else. When I wrote the tiger story in chapter one, I was looking for a story to capture the idea that life-or-death, back-against-the-wall, no-other-alternative situations tend to force us to perform at our peak. Like the young monk who was pushed to his full potential by the charging tiger, I found that hiring my first employee with a limited budget only lit a bigger fire under me to hustle for business. And it forced me to focus on the actions that were directly related to business development, rather than anything that wasn't.

I wanted to replicate what I'd done in the martial arts motion capture studio. Specifically, I wanted to give my customers what they wanted, the way they wanted it, and at the price they wanted. This is a very tall order for anyone.

Some may argue that building an army early on in the side hustle journey is too soon. Think about it—most side hustlers are just starting out, and accepting this burden so early may be too much.

I understand and respect this argument. However, I respectfully disagree.

You should always be recruiting and team building. Always. One of the amazing benefits of side hustling is the mobility. You are so small that you are nimble enough to jump on opportunities when they arise.

You need to have a bullpen of resources you can turn to in the event you stumble across an opportunity.

You should know that when you are at the side hustle stage, you do not necessarily have to hire someone full-time with benefits. You can offer part-time positions or ask someone to collaborate on specific projects as an independent contractor, which would greatly limit your risk.

The project-based approach allows you to test out team chemistry and deliverables. You can team up with the most talented people in the world, but if they don't perform when you need them, they are like a beautiful car with no engine.

When I assembled a team for a big action video game project, none of those people were my full-time employees. They were all independent contractors for one project. However, I knew where to look when I needed to assemble the team.

The trick is finding talented teammates, which is difficult.

In my law side hustle, I really struggled with finding talented teammates because I had to compete with big companies that were also recruiting talent.

I started with a number of recruiting services. Surprisingly, most of the candidates looked down on me. I was a small company. Most of the recruiters and candidates did not give me much attention.

Next, I turned my attention to my network. Again, no luck.

I hit a wall. I tried to get in the minds of all the people who turned me down so I could better understand their position.

It totally made sense. Why would anyone go with me? I was an unstable side hustle. I thought back on the reason I was side hustling in the first place. I hated my job and the way my company treated me.

I turned my focus to people who really hated their jobs. Turns out, there was a massive pool of people in that category.

I can relate to hating my job. I hated my job, but why? Well, there were a lot of reasons, but two of them seemed universal. First, I was capped on how much I could make. Second, I had to commute two hours a day on a crowded train to get to and from work.

These were two huge pain points that so many people were dealing with. So to start recruiting, I gave people the option to work from home and offered an option to work for performance-based bonuses.

Back then, the work-from-home option was very unusual and attracted so many people. People hate sitting in traffic or riding on a crowded train. Not only was I offering work, but I was offering to restore wasted commuting time to their day. I was giving people back their time, which is huge. Especially to someone with kids.

I was shocked at how many people were interested. I now had my talent pool to choose from. I hired someone part-time, with the goal of bringing them on full-time within six months. That was fair to the employee and gave me a long enough lead time and a reasonable goal.

See how I started with the employee's needs and found a way to solve their problem? After I solved their problem, I aligned it with my goal.

At six months, that employee moved to full-time, and I brought on a second assistant part-time, with the same goal. And every six months after that, I repeated this cycle and slowly created a team.

With each new hire, I identified one more administrative, back-office-type task and permanently transferred that job from me to the new person—which freed me even more to focus on revenue-generating work.

When you first start your side hustle, you will deploy a significant amount of your resources to marketing in order to get dollars in the door.

At the side hustle level, cash flow is like oxygen to your company. You are not some big organization with a huge balance sheet that can absorb losses. You are a side hustle, and you need cash flow. When I started, I placed all the teammates I hired in operations.

I was generous with what I learned. My goal was simple: to make my employees as good as or better than me at the job. If people could focus on specific jobs, they would eventually become better than me. Just like my wushu teammates were all better than me at something, my side hustle teammates would become better than me at something.

What did I look for in that first hire (and the second and third)? A few things.

First, I'll tell you what I didn't especially care about: what they already knew how to do. I believe that today almost everyone can learn almost everything. With free information, tutorials, and software-as-a-service technology solutions, skills are easier to teach than ever before. I jokingly tell people I can teach anyone to make a basic balance sheet (but it's true).

Historically, knowledge was a huge barrier of entry for side hustlers, but with the internet providing free content at our fingertips, that barrier has been for the most part broken down.

But what can't be taught? Character. Competitiveness. Hunger. These are the traits I look for in every new hire.

You can teach a kid a martial arts technique, but if they do not have the hunger to practice it when no one is looking, they are not going to be the best at it. Especially in team atmospheres, work ethic is more important than talent.

Even with that first hire, you should think in terms of a team, because you're eventually going to have one. You're seeking potential teammates when you hire. Just as in sports, focus on character and chemistry. The best player with the wrong attitude can destroy everything. A person with the right character will be patient enough to learn everything they need in order to do the job and will work hard.

You are also going to need a person who is flexible. You'll frequently encounter new issues and problems in your side hustle, and you need to be confident that your employee can run with whatever it is you throw their way. The world thrives on problem solvers, not paper pushers. Seek out a true problem solver for your team.

You may not be able to pay your assistant much at the beginning. But you can still make that person feel important. Describe the clear path to success that they can follow if they stay with you. You'll be shocked at how loyal people become when they are treated well and if you follow through with the payoff you promise.

If you possibly can, try to hire at least one new person each year. This brings in fresh perspective and new energy—both of which will help you expand even further. Too many managers take a passive approach and think about hiring only to replace someone who leaves. I learned this lesson from watching a mentor, one of the greatest trial lawyers I ever met. Unfortunately, he got sick, and because he had nobody in place to help his firm continue when he was not around, his business failed.

Executives at many companies will tell you they strive to be customer-centric. Well, I believe in that too. But I actually think of my employees as customers—they are every bit as important as the clients who pay us money for our services. I'm paying them to grow my company. So I've built our business around the needs of both external and internal customers—but the needs of my employees, my internal customers, come first.

Yes, I'm serious: *to build a customer-centric company, you must take care of your employees first.* You must help them reach their financial goals. You must understand their evolving needs.

You also have to listen to your employees. Besides trying to keep them happy, you should treat them as the frontline ears for your customers' voices. You need your employees talking to you.

If your employees are happy, they will inevitably see to it that your external customers are happy too.

The story of Xiaoda is the underlying philosophy of my company, and it's the first thing I tell other business leaders when I'm asked for advice. It's a generous give-first approach to business, and it works.

It takes a lot of discipline to make sure your people are taken care of first. But if you are generous with your employees, they are more likely to overperform. And when they overperform, your customers will be happy and your business will grow. It really is as simple as that.

CUSTOMERS AND CLIENTS

Now that you have a pool of teammates in place who can help you take advantage of new opportunities, you need to have a community of potential customers who will mobilize if a service or product that solves their problems is offered. The next aspect to building your army is your customers and clients.

I understand the confusion. How could customers and clients be part of your army? Good question. Historically, a company offered a product or service, then advertised to potential customers, because it had a captive audience. The reason it had a captive audience is that there were only so many television stations a person could watch. A company just made sure its commercials were on one of those stations.

Today there is so much noise out there in so many alternative mediums of communication that no one has a captive audience anymore.

Instead, developing customers and clients through community building has become a huge part of contemporary business. Your customers must feel like they are part of that community.

It gets even more complicated.

Historically, customers and clients paid a business money in exchange for goods or services. Today, the customer experience reigns supreme. Customers are more educated today than ever before. They influence and interact with a business on multiple levels. Social proof and community engagement are far more prevalent. Social proof is a fancy way of saying "word of mouth." People tend to trust their friends when it comes to recommendations.

Think about it. People often befriend those with whom they are compatible, so recommendations tend to be in line with that same compatibility. When someone leaves an online review or recommends you, they are staking their personal reputation that you will deliver. That is huge!

Customers and clients now have a lot more power and influence.

Ultimately, it's the role of your side hustle to solve a problem for someone, right? And not only to solve the problem but to solve it in the way your customer or client wants it solved. Do it right, and they'll tell all their friends and family. Do it wrong, and you'll never see them again. Or worse, they'll try to tell the world.

> Customer expectation has risen to incredible heights. If you treat a customer well, they will become a sort of brand ambassador and tell the world. If you treat a customer poorly, they will become a brand assassin and tell the world.

I really got this wrong when I first started my side hustle. I was focused on my own story, my own brand. I thought all I had to do was tell people I was a unique, martial arts–practicing lawyer. I thought people would want to do business with me because I was so cool.

This was not the case.

In fact, people were interested in my martial arts background—but only when I clearly explained how what I'd learned in martial arts would enable me to create solutions that would make their lives better. If I was cool, that was just the parsley to the real steak and potatoes—the actual solution.

Your clients' needs are going to evolve over time. How they want your solution delivered is going to evolve too. You have to constantly track what they need and innovate ways to deliver it.

> **Your side hustle needs to be a tool that improves the customer's journey, not yours.**

The best way to do all this is captured in the Japanese phrase *genchi genbutsu*, which translates to "go see for yourself." You have to go experience what the client is experiencing in order to know if you're solving problems the way the client needs them to be solved. This requires two-way communication, with an emphasis on listening, not talking, especially when you ask directly, "How can I make your life easier?"

Just as with your employees, your job is to explain to your customers their path to success and how you will get them there. If you can do this repeatedly over time, you will create happy customers who in turn will become brand ambassadors for you and your business.

My philosophy of developing brand ambassadors revolves around creating an educated customer through relevant content. Most people sense a lack of control in many areas of their lives—time, traffic, the weather, and so on all seem to be out of their personal control. By contrast, I emphasize giving a client enough information, enough knowledge of the factors to consider, to be able to feel in control of a decision. Rather than dictate a solution, it's far more effective to guide the client to the best decision. Even when the decision is the same one I would have chosen (and if I'm guiding the client properly, it generally is), by giving the client a sense of control, I dramatically increase their satisfaction. And a satisfied customer is a customer who tells their friends positive things about you. This social proof is the best marketing you will ever get.

Depending on your business, you may need to adjust for friction and costs. Some businesses simply streamline processes, to eliminate friction and push down costs. That's okay sometimes, but not always.

For example, for some services I provide, like creating a power of attorney, my process is frictionless and low cost. That's because the service is a commodity that most any lawyer can provide.

But for other services that are more personal and more important to the client, I will create deliberate friction at certain points of the process in order to catch things and involve the client. If you get too many clients needing high-touch work, you can't effectively deliver that personal touch. So for these services, rather than lower the cost, I charge a premium rate—which decreases the number of clients while increasing revenue.

MENTORS

The final step in creating your army is finding mentors. You need to be able to mobilize mentors when needed.

As a side hustler, you will be nimble—you will be closer to customers so you can forecast consumer behavior trends, and highly adaptable to new opportunities.

However, side hustlers need mentors because sometimes the opportunities that arise will have complexities that the side hustler may not be able to manage alone.

One mentor in particular took me under his wing. He was a well-known lawyer, and many younger lawyers wanted to be trained by him. He threw me out of his office several times, but I was persistent.

Finally, when he retired, he agreed to help me. He called and said he'd teach me everything he knew. In the span of a year, he drilled his forty years of experience into me, usually in conversations in a coffee shop.

He helped me get my side hustle up and running, and with my new-found knowledge I began to become formidable. Early on, I snagged a case against a very famous lawyer, the kind you see on TV all the time. I was terrified.

I had no idea what I was doing, but this was an incredible opportunity for me. I called my mentor, who was very well versed in this area.

My mentor met me at the coffee shop and guided me through the process from behind the scenes. And in the end? I won. I got this famous TV lawyer to submit and retreat.

When I called my mentor to tell him, I kept getting his voicemail. I wanted to thank him, to tell him that his strategy had worked, but he never called back.

Finally, his family called me. He'd died of cancer. His daughter told me that as he was dying, he saw my call, but his tongue had ceased functioning. He passed away shortly thereafter.

At his funeral, there was an army of lawyers he had quietly been training, all there to grieve. I was his last student. If you have a mentor, tell them how much you appreciate them. I carry the burden of not telling him, and it haunts me.

Build your business with urgency, and help all those who ask. Kindness is just good business.

TRUST

A huge part of your success will depend on the people you surround yourself with.

How do you go about building a strong, growing, happy community? By building trust and connection.

In martial arts, sparring is supposed to be light-contact combat in the form of striking or grappling. Generally, you are not going 100 percent. Instead, you try to match the intensity of your opponent. Hopefully, you both go strong enough to get your repetitions in, but light enough not to hurt each other. If someone goes too hard, things escalate quickly.

Why is this such a sensitive process? Vulnerability. You are allowing yourself to be vulnerable to allow the other to get their practice in. If they are not conscious of your vulnerability (that is, if they are selfish and go too hard), they can hurt you with a punch, kick, or joint lock. For this to work, you need to trust your training partner not to cross the line.

The exact same concept exists in business. Your customers are vulnerable. They need to trust you.

Business comes down to trust. Your customers are drowning in advertising and have access to endless amounts of information. Do they trust you to solve their problems? Do they feel connected enough to you? If so, that sense of trust and connection cuts through the noise, which is a relief to your customers.

How can you build trust? I'll tell you how I did it. Start by building a community.

As a general rule, I spend a third of my time with peers my own age, a third of my time with people a generation younger than me, and a third of my time with people older (and generally more successful) than me.

Peers: I believe healthy competition is good—it creates a balanced ecosystem. So my competitors are not my enemies. Even sharing best practices with them is not a bad thing; you can learn a lot from competitors, and it's okay for them to learn from you. Don't give away your secret sauce, of course. But there's a lot to be gained from cultivating relationships with your peers.

It's also good for your peers to see that you are at the top of your game and confident, but also have boots on the ground and are constantly seeking information and a competitive edge. If the king of the jungle strays too far away, another would-be king comes sniffing around. It's better to let everyone know the king is here and in charge.

The next generation: I enjoy spending time with potential apprentices—not just to be able to spot and recruit new young talent, but to learn and understand their perspective.

Just because something has been done one way for thirty years does not make it the right way today, or for the future. Change is inevitable, and those who accelerate change will participate in the upswing of an emerging market (and those who do not will experience the roller-coaster plunge of an aging, maturing market). The younger generation just sees things differently from me—and helps me see things others in my generation are missing.

The older generation: Spending time with people older and more successful than you is important. First, you learn ways to be successful. Second, often you'll be able to catch some of the overflow they cannot capture themselves. If people know you, trust you, and start seeing your value, they will start giving you opportunities. I began my career hanging out with people in the twilight of their careers (and lives). Their perspective helped me understand early on what is important: family, friends, love. All the successes of these older mentors meant very little to them after a certain point.

We covered a lot in this chapter, but the main takeaway is that you need to be capable of mobilizing your army when opportunities arise. Your army consists of your employees, your customers and clients, and your mentors. The way you build this army is with trust and connection.

PRACTICE TIP
Your First Teammate

What follows is focused on your first teammate—the very beginning of your team. *Teammate* can be defined as someone you hire as an employee, a partner, or a project-based independent contractor.
How do you start?

1. **Try to understand the pain point of the potential teammate.** I don't mean money, because increased income alone will not work over time. If you are a mean person, then your teammate will leave you once they are financially stable. What is this person's pain point, and how can you solve it for them? Put yourself in their shoes. What can you offer them to join you?

> Create a definitive path to success in a nurturing environment that cures a pain point.

2. **Solve that pain point.** As an up-and-coming side hustler, you are a risky bet for anyone, because you may go out of business due to cash flow issues. You have to offer something strong enough to overcome your potential collaborators' fears. For example, when I was hiring part-time employees, I offered to solve the problem of time poverty. I wanted to eliminate the time loss and stress of the work commute. I saved my people two hours each day. This time savings was a strong enough reason for them to overcome their concerns about my initial instability. If your side hustle allows, offer the same or something else that makes you different.

3. **Show a path to success.** A huge problem with companies is that they have glass ceilings. (In my world we refer to "bamboo ceilings," which limit the growth of Asians in business. Don't believe it's real? Go check out how many Asian lawyers are partners at law firms.) I physically draw out a graph for each of my team members showing the skills I expect from them and the rewards for hitting those targets.

4. **Create a nurturing environment.** Do not be a jerk to your employees. Do not allow your customers to be mean to your employees.

Here's a hypothetical example. Let's say you've launched a lawn-mowing side hustle. There are a lot of lawns out there, and you can only do so many. So how would you find employees to help, so you can spend more time growing the business? Consider trying the following:

1. Find people in your network who work nights and are sick of working nights. With landscaping, you have to work during the day, because if you do it too late, the neighbors complain.
2. Find people who are sick of being stuck indoors in a cubicle all day. Landscaping work is an opportunity for these people to work outside.

See what I did there? I started with the pain point of the potential hire, then backed into your side hustle as a possible solution.

Next, show the person how you would solve this pain point, and illustrate a path to success for this teammate. For example, "Hey, get out of that cubicle and come work for me outside. It is hard work, but if you work with me for two years, I will show you everything I know. Then you can either stay or go start your own company in a different territory." Along with simply treating the person well, you can make your offer attractive by providing a bridge to their own future side hustle.

Sound crazy?

That is a real-life side hustle success story of the landscaping company that mows my lawn. For his first hire, my landscaper struggled to find help via the traditional recruiting avenues. So he focused on people who were just sick of working in a cubicle. Today he has a seven-figure company with apprentices who are franchising his name all over.

CHAPTER 3 ☯ TIME

*The third step of the Tao of the side
hustle is to gain control of the most
valuable resource in your life: time.*

YOUR MOST VALUABLE RESOURCE IN LIFE AND BUSINESS
is time.

Period. End of story.

If you lose money, you can make it back. Time can never be recouped.
This was a true "aha" moment for me.

Chapter two focused on building your army. One major reason you
need an army is to free up your time.

Think about it. There are basically only three aspects of a side hustle business: production, distribution, and marketing. But when all three
of those are your responsibility, there's almost never enough time to do
everything you should be doing.

In addition, business moves fast and you must always be learning and
looking for new opportunities. You cannot do all this if you are working
alone. You need teammates who can help free up your time.

I learned this lesson the hard way.

I had two major film projects under my belt. Then for several years my only side hustle was real estate closings. People saw my name in the video game credits, which got me some attention and increased the exposure of my law practice.

I was still working in the job I hated, but things started to pick up in my side hustle to the point where I was not living hand to mouth anymore. And then something crazy happened. I was asked to do the motion capture for my third big studio project.

Sounds like a blessing, right? Well, yes and no. I had way too much on my plate. I had stretched myself too thin. I did not know how to say no to opportunities.

There was not enough time in the day for me to do all three. I was running around trying to do one job while the other two were pulling me in different directions. I was exhausted.

Worse, I did not have time to train, and I got out of shape.

Before this third project, I had always thought of myself as being really good at martial arts. In fact, in my mind, my last project had been my peak performance.

It quickly became apparent that this time was different, however. I was now thirty-five years old. I was now training less because I was working all the time. The studio brought in athletes in their early twenties. All they did was work out.

I looked around and realized I was the oldest and slowest person in the motion capture studio. It had only been seven years since I was on the US Wushu Team. But trust me—I really stuck out in the tight spandex motion capture suit. I was filming this huge project surrounded by world-class athletes. I did not perform well. I was outclassed.

In a young person's world, I had gotten old. I left this project feeling depressed because, like the sands of time, my youth had just slipped through my fingers. It took this event to really make me understand it.

Needless to say, I was not entirely happy with my performance. I do not think the bosses at the studio were either.

Nothing is more valuable than time. Without it, you are not improving. Without it, you are standing still and the world will pass you by, just as the younger, fitter fighters passed me by.

After I realized this truth, I did everything possible to not only free up my time but move with an extreme sense of urgency in everything I did. I began living my life as if it could end at any moment. Because it can.

I started prioritizing the things that needed to get done. I decided I would happily trade money for time, by hiring people to take things off my plate. I would then reinvest this time to continue searching for new frontiers or side hustles.

Real estate closings were a great side hustle, but they were not my endgame. I wanted more out of life. But for me to get more, I needed time so I could focus on improvement.

There was once a famous scholar who had accomplished much but had never discovered the true meaning of life.

Was it wisdom? Was it wealth? The scholar had amassed a great deal of each.

Yet still the scholar felt empty.

So the scholar decided to seek the answer from one much smarter than him: the dragon spirit that lived at the top of the mountain. The dragon spirit was guardian of the bridge to the riches of the spirit world and represented power, wealth, and luck.

The only way for the scholar to reach the top of the mountain was by reaching inner peace through meditation.

Decades passed, with the scholar meditating and seeking inner peace . . . but unfortunately failing to reach the top of the mountain. Day and night the scholar would practice meditation, searching for the meaning of life, and day and night he failed. He pleaded with heaven and earth for a path.

Finally, the dragon spirit heard his calls and agreed to see the scholar. During meditation, the dragon appeared and shouted, "WHY HAVE YOU COME HERE? WE ALLOW YOU HERE JUST TO SILENCE YOUR CRIES!"

The scholar, terrified, asked, "Why am I here? What is the meaning of life?"

This angered the dragon. "WHY ASK SUCH FOOLISH QUES-TIONS?" the dragon roared. "DOES THE BABY ASK WHY IT BREATHES OR THE SUN WHY IT SHINES? DO NOT ASK. JUST DO!"

The scholar was visibly frustrated.

The dragon spirit turned and yelled, "THE HUMAN WORLD HAS TURNED WEAK. PEOPLE ARE ENTITLED; THEY EXPECT EVERY-THING WITH NO PATIENCE. THEY WANT US TO GIVE THEM THE ANSWERS WITHOUT SEARCHING FOR THEMSELVES."

The scholar asked again, "What is the meaning of life? Why are we here?" And so on.

The dragon, enraged, shouted, "ENOUGH QUESTIONS. HERE IS YOUR ANSWER!"

The dragon's eyes turned blood red and he rose and roared a flame of fire.

The scholar stood up and ran down the mountain with the dragon just on his heels. With every spit of fire and flame, the dragon just missed the scholar. The chase continued until the scholar came to a cliff.

The view was amazing, the sun shone on his face, and the cool breeze kissed his skin. The water below was breathtaking. But . . . the dragon was coming to eat him, and there was nowhere left to run.

The dragon flew close to the scholar and spit out a great flame. The scholar felt heat engulf his entire body.

In that instant, his whole life flashed before his eyes. But what did he see? Only the faces of his two daughters.

Why had he wasted so much time? Why had he spent his life pur-suing goals, making money, searching for the meaning of life? He could have spent it with his family. The meaning of life was simply to live life! It really was that simple. These were his last thoughts as his body was consumed by fire, his skin melted, and his bones cracked in the flames.

Suddenly, the scholar woke from his meditation. He never asked himself the question again. He simply got up, went to his daughters, and focused on living his best life.

Stop wasting time on things that do not matter. Like the fire in the story, time wasters can consume your life. Time is your most valuable resource and you must only invest it in things that are bringing you what you want.

In Japanese, *kensho* (in a Buddhist context) loosely translates to "discovery." I experienced my first *kensho* when I realized the importance of time. It was reinforced when my mentors began dying around me.

You know how in the old-school kung fu movies our hero must seek out the tutelage of an old, wise—but harsh—teacher to learn secret kung fu techniques? Well, I took this really seriously. I sought out older kung fu masters to help guide me on my journey. And it really worked. Until they started to involuntarily leave me.

Losing them taught me again how valuable time is; when I learned that lesson, the lack of time became the most important problem to solve.

> The Chinese characters 四山 (*sì shān*) denote a Buddhist phrase that loosely translated means "Birth, age, sickness, and death are like four mountains closing in on you." One thing we know for sure is that we are not getting out of this thing alive. So you might as well maximize every moment here.

Have you ever felt like there are just not enough minutes in a day? That no matter what you do, you can't keep up with your responsibilities at either work or home? Most of us know this feeling. And if we're parents, well, that's pretty much how we feel 24/7.

Guess what? *Our customers feel the same way.* So in my business, I focus a lot on helping my customers save time.

Here we will focus on three key ways to save time: time allocation and management, execution, and delegation.

A friend of mine once passed along a popular self-help book. I read it with an open mind, but as I got into it, I realized that very little of it was realistic. One of the book's suggestions was to take extremely long periods of time to meditate.

I thought to myself, "Where in the world would I get hours to sit around and meditate?" (All you parents with full-time jobs, I know you hear me on this. Sure, just put aside six hours to meditate. It's not like you need to get the kids dressed and ready for school!)

In martial arts and business, knowing that time is the most precious resource I must preserve, here's how I do it.

TIME ALLOCATION AND MANAGEMENT

Time allocation is prioritizing the work you are going to spend time on and completing tasks in the allotted time, no excuses.

You cannot win all wars or make everyone happy, but you can be very strategic and deliberate about which wars you will enter.

Managing "what gets done and when" became incredibly important to me. If your friends, family, or network give you an opportunity, you still need to deliver. You have to prioritize and execute.

You have to eliminate things that do not advance your goals and objectives. We started this chapter with a story of a scholar who asked way too many questions that did not matter. He asked so many questions that he had a vision that a dragon's fire consumed him.

When you are trying to get your side hustle up and running, you will feel like you are getting pulled in so many different directions. Over time, as you win your time back, you can bring back things that are important to you. For now, you have to get your base stable.

Pick what gets done based on importance and urgency.

After about four years into my side hustle, I started to make a little bit of money. Not enough to quit my job, but enough to see that the side hustle might become something. The problem was that there were only so many hours in a day, and I was stretched too thin. I was running to work, then running to the side hustle, then running to my home life. I had to cut out the fat.

At my full-time job, I did just enough to not get noticed and not get fired. Every spare ounce of energy I had went into the side hustle. I prioritized the most urgent tasks and blocked out my schedule every morning.

To be clear, at this point in my life, I cut out anything that did not further my side hustle.

> At some point you will need to make the
> decision to prioritize your side hustle. Only
> you can tell when that time is right.

Training in martial arts was no longer my top priority. I was in survival mode, and I needed to focus on making money. I did the unthinkable for me—I stopped consistently training. This was devastating to me. Martial arts was my form of meditation and defined who I was.

However, I needed to temporarily prioritize my full-time job and side hustle over my personal life. You will likely be forced to do the same.

Time management entails blocking off time to do work.

At first, working on a laptop in my basement, I performed every single task necessary for my side hustle. You're probably going to be in the same boat initially. Every email that came in; every aspect of marketing, production, and distribution; every administrative task—when you are a one-person business, there's nobody to delegate to. Especially if you're still working a nine-to-five gig, trust me, it will be enough to drive you crazy.

There is too much to manage for you to do this all in your head. You have to set up a system that tracks your time. Many lawyers are forced to track their time down to five-minute increments with billing systems.

Tracking five-minute increments is probably too intense for most people, but tracking hourly increments is doable for all.

Your phone makes tracking your daily schedule easier than ever, but even if you don't use your phone to do so, make sure you do it somewhere. Whether you do it on your phone or on a physical calendar, write it down. You should start your day by blocking off time. Eventually you will be able to stretch this out to your day, week, and month.

EXECUTION

Whatever obstacles you face, you have to get it done—no excuses. If someone gives you an opportunity, you had better deliver, or it will be the last opportunity you get. Like our earlier story, do not let the dragon fire distract you. Stay focused on executing your priorities.

If I was going to give up martial arts, I was not going to play around. There is zero room for procrastination when you have a full-time job and are trying to get a side hustle going. When you sit down to work, turn off your phone and get to work. Get rid of TV and social media for a while and focus on this.

My schedule was packed. I woke at 5 AM, and from 5 to 7 AM I did side hustle work. From 7 to 9 AM, I got the kids up and out and got myself to my day job. From 9 AM to noon, I did my job; then I spent lunch hour with side hustle clients and spent the afternoon back at the day job. Finally, I went home for dinner, spent some time with my wife and kids, and then got back on the phone to hunt for business. Go to sleep, rinse, repeat.

Yes, it absolutely was a grind. But it was also great. Because literally, week by week, I could sense that the side hustle was going to turn into something bigger. And by approaching my schedule that way, I accomplished a few useful things.

One, I made the work predictable. I knew I had the exact same parameters each day, so I didn't have to overthink what I was going to do at any given moment. I already knew and could just go ahead and execute my tasks. I tried to eliminate anything that would disrupt this predictability.

Two, I knew I had to be super focused to fit everything into those short windows of time. Sure, sometimes I got up even earlier or did some of the work in the evening. But for the most part, compartmentalizing tasks in this way made me way more productive in each of the segments.

Three, I made my schedule predictable for others. The people around me—and at first this meant only my amazing wife—understood what I was doing and when I was doing it. My wife was completely on board with what I was trying to launch, but we were also co-parenting two kids. Dedicating specific time slots to specific tasks meant we didn't have to renegotiate things like childcare every day. As I started to bring on part-time assistants, they knew exactly when I would be available and when not to try to reach me.

After a while these double shifts started to take their toll on me.

I realized that instead of being stuck in a financial trap, now I was stuck in a *time* trap too!

This is not a sustainable model. So early on, I promised myself an escape plan.

DELEGATION

In many ways, chapters two and three of this book blend together. In chapter two, we talked about building an army, and part of building that army is hiring employees. The reason this is so critical is that you need to delegate tasks that need to get done. But you need to find the critical points in your business where you must deploy your personal time.

When I was in my late teens, my martial arts coach made me teach the kids' class. At first, I thought it was cool, because it gave me an opportunity to show off. However, I quickly discovered the downside: in order to teach the kids' class, I needed to keep showing up. If I was not there, then there was no class. This was a big problem for me, because if I was teaching, that meant I was not drilling or learning new techniques to improve my game.

I decided I was going to teach some of the other students so they could take over teaching the class. When a few of them were good enough, I gave them the majority of my wages to cover my classes. This freed up my time, allowing me to train more and get better. I took this concept with me through life, and it is one of the reasons I am constantly teaching.

I started saving all the income I was earning from my law side hustle. I didn't spend it to cover living expenses or pay off credit card balances; I kept it in a separate account and chose to reinvest it in the business.

The idea was, I would hire a person to take care of non-revenue-generating tasks, so that I would have more time for revenue-generating tasks. Sounds simple, right?

The tricky part is deciding what those tasks are and delegating the right ones. So, big picture, there are three basics areas for side hustles: marketing, production, and distribution.

I needed to delegate, but where should I start? For me, the answer was to start delegating parts of production. I wanted to control all parts of customer interaction so that if there was a problem, I could immediately step in.

Most customer interaction occurs in marketing and distribution. Hello and goodbye. Focusing on these two parts allowed me to build deeper relationships with customers and in turn get more customers, which in turn created more revenue.

Most importantly, I invested much of the time the delegation freed up into improving my skills.

Delegation should look like this:

Step 1: You find a product or service to offer and become great at it. This is all you.

Step 2: You break down the side hustle to marketing, production, and distribution. You teach a teammate to take over production as much as possible.

Step 3: You focus on marketing and distribution to keep contact with the customer. Any free time should be used for improvement and research and for development of new opportunities.

Time allocation—and allocation of responsibilities across your team—is dynamic. You should be evaluating frequently what you are spending your time on, and reallocating responsibilities across your team accordingly (even if that team is just you and one part-time assistant). Optimize for growth, not short-term revenue—you want this thing to grow.

> When you start your side hustle, so much of your time is spent on getting customers in the door. You need that cash flow to survive. As your business starts to stabilize, however, you will move your attention to the quality of your production.

PRACTICE TIP
Time Ninja

The most important resource of this path, this Tao of the side hustle, is time. Time is the oxygen to the lungs, or the blood to the heart. You must be present and conscious of time with the highest level of commitment.

We cannot make more time, but we can protect and preserve it. Consider this approach:

Step 1: Start saying no! You have to either remove all unproductive activity, convert unproductive activity, or strategically multitask.

If you decide that pursuing a side hustle is a possibility for you, then do the following:

- **Remove unproductive activity:** You have to get rid of all the personal time drains. Get rid of time-wasting activities. If your side hustle includes video games and social media, then great, keep using them to the extent that they promote the side hustle. However, if you are using video games and social media for personal use not connected to the side hustle, drop them. If you truly love these activities, you can return to them when you get back your time.
- **Convert unproductive activity:** If you are using social media to mindlessly scroll, stop it. On the other hand, if you can use social media to learn how to give your brand exposure, do it with that goal in mind.
- **Strategically multitask:** I generally listen to podcasts and audiobooks when I work out and drive. I consume information at an incredible rate now. You need to learn everything about your profession. You need to know both history and what the thought leaders of today are saying.

Step 2: Get up earlier or stay up later. When you are starting your side hustle, you need time to focus. I have two young daughters. I need to get up and get everything done before they wake up. Once they are up, it is game over and they take over my life. So I wake up at 5 AM. Work on your side hustle before anyone gets up.

Step 3: You must set and enforce a schedule. The easiest way to do this is on your cell phone calendar. Create habits every day. If you are balancing your side hustle with a full-time job, you have to schedule all client interactions in very specific time slots. Seek customers who are able to interact in these specific time slots.

If the above sounds like I'm asking you to find and invest even more time, that's true. But if you do it right, you'll eventually earn all of it back.

CHAPTER 4 TREASURE

The fourth step of the Tao of the side
hustle is to build your treasure. Cash flow
is like oxygen to a business. Let's get some
air in our lungs and start breathing.

YOU MUST NURTURE YOUR BUSINESS AS IF YOU ARE NUR-
turing a garden.

Nature gives you some rain sometimes, but when it doesn't, you still need to water the plants. The same concept applies in business: while you are starting, you may have a good month, but that does not mean you will have another good month.

For most of my life I had been a failure at things, but I had been successful at martial arts motion capture, and that was really special. So the last, disappointing experience, in which I felt too old around younger athletes, brought me to an important fork in the road.

I was depressed about how the last filming had gone, but I was also motivated. This side hustle changed my mentality, and the exposure I got from it helped my real estate closings side hustle. There was a market segment (people who play video games, watch animated movies, or are martial arts fans) that started to notice me. I was able to leverage this exposure. When meeting clients, I would use it as a way for people to remember me.

I was not making a huge profit, but the side hustle was really starting to work. I took from it only enough money for a super-basic lifestyle. I invested almost every available dime after expenses back into the side hustle by hiring people. I mean this very literally.

A side hustle is a business. When a cash-basis business has a profit, however big or small, the money saved is considered to be retained earnings. Retained earnings are basically a savings account for your profits. Most people distribute their retained earnings to themselves to pay for their personal lives.

There is absolutely nothing wrong with this, especially when you are established. However, I put my retained earnings back into my side hustle business.

When I started, the side hustle did not make much money. But in my mind, it was an appreciable asset. I wanted to grow it. If I took those earnings for personal use, I would just waste them. By putting them back into the business, the business kept growing.

It was a couple of years before I began to take any income from the side hustle. But at just about this point—even as I was depressed about possibly losing the motion capture side hustle—I realized there was enough profit in the real estate closings side hustle to enable me to earn the same income that I could from my full-time job.

At that point I had a decision to make: keep on splitting my days between day job and side hustle, thus limiting the growth of the hustle, or quit my day job and focus full-time on the new business.

Guess what I did?

I punted.

I told my boss at the day job what I wanted to do, and I asked if I could go part-time. I just wasn't quite ready for the risk of eliminating that guaranteed income. (Actually, back then, people's biggest concern when leaving a job was losing their health insurance, something the Affordable Care Act thankfully has removed as an obstacle.)

But—and I'll always be grateful for this—the executives at my day job weren't too keen on the idea. They liked me, but only as a full-time worker.

In the previous chapter, I mentioned that there will come a point when you need to prioritize your side hustle. I said that only you would know that time. Well, this was when I knew I had to make my side hustle my full-time job.

They wouldn't go for the part-time arrangement. They didn't like the idea of me breaking free. They said no.

Like I said, I'm actually grateful they said no. It just accelerated everything. It made me do what I should have been doing in the first place.

I quit, and I put everything I had into making my new business grow. I quit being an employee of my full-time day job and became an employee of my side hustle.

When I look back on it now, I understand that a lot of employers are like this. They don't mind that you make just enough to stay afloat—actually, they prefer it. That way, you'll never leave.

They aren't willing to take the handcuffs off. *You* have to do that yourself.

I quit my job on the spot, and I started working full-time on my side hustle.

I was making enough that I was able to eliminate the trap of a full-time day job. No more wasting two hours every day in a commute, no more mandatory overtime on weekends, no more face time in the office that felt mandatory. All the time sinks that come with a job—most of

which we don't even notice or question, because we're so used to them—
were gone in an instant.

However, my family and I were far from financially secure. We still
had to live very simply.

Once each year—on the fifteenth day of the seventh month of the lunar calendar—the spirit world and the human world merge. This is known as Ghost Night. On this night you must honor your ancestors by offering them a seat at your table and feasting in their honor.

As legend has it, there is a place where you can actually walk over into the spirit world to speak to your ancestors: the Shinto Bridge, deep in the haunted Kami Forest. However—and this is a big "however"— the Shinto Bridge is hidden. And the only way to find it is though the guidance of the bridge's guardian, a trickster spirit named Okami.

Okami likes to take the form of a fox. He loves tricking humans. He'll provide passage over the Shinto Bridge, but only to those who first pass several tests.

Every year on Ghost Night, several brave souls inevitably enter the Kami Forest in search of Okami. And every year, they are never seen or heard from again.

On one particular Ghost Night, there were three who sought passage to the spirit world: Dae, Young, and Paek. Dae was a banker; Young, a politician; and Paek, a teacher.

At midnight Okami appeared to the three as a giant fox roaming the forest. Okami said, "I will cross you over to the spirit world, but only those who pass three challenges shall cross." The three men nodded in agreement.

Okami guided them to a giant castle made of sand, in the middle of which were unbelievable riches of gold and jewelry. Okami said, "You will need a gold coin to pass over to the spirit world. Go, and take one coin. I urge you not to be greedy."

The three men entered the castle. As on a beach, their feet dug into the sand with each step. They reached the middle, and each man grabbed a gold coin . . . but Dae filled his pockets with more gold, then took off his shirt, filled it with gold, and slung it over his shoulder like a sack.

As they tried to leave, heavier than they had entered, the sand began to suck them in. Dae sank quickly. Paek reached for Dae, offering his hand—but Dae refused to take it, because he could not let go of the gold. Dae disappeared into the sand.

Paek and Young ran outside in time to hear Okami say, "Just as in life, Dae allowed riches to bury him." Okami motioned for the two men to follow him. They approached two long canoes, each with three seats—a seat for a man in the middle, a seat for a water dragon in front, and a seat for a fire dragon in back. They paid a demon spirit with the gold coins and set out in their respective canoes.

"Listen to both dragons," Okami said. "They are both here to guide you."

Both men began to paddle, and the dragons began to advise them on how to navigate the waters. Unfortunately, Young had been raised by the Fire Clan; he hated the Water Clan, so each time the water dragon tried to give a direction, Young ignored it. Soon, Young decided he didn't even want to sit near the water dragon and moved back to sit next to the fire dragon at the end of the canoe.

When the water became choppy, the canoe was not balanced. It flipped over, and Young sank into the water and drowned.

Paek listened to both dragons and made it across the river. Okami was waiting for him there and said, "Balance is important. If the weight of your opinion is too one-sided, your boat will eventually tip over. Listen to others. That does not mean you must agree with them, but that hearing their opinion gives you perspective."

Paek nodded, and Okami looked hard at him. "It is now just you, and only one challenge remains. To reach the spirit world, you must cross the invisible Shinto Bridge. May I ask why you want to cross?"

Paek said, "I simply want a moment to thank my parents. Rather than give me a bowl of rice, they taught me how to grow my own rice. I have dedicated my life to helping others grow their own rice. Money and politics come and go, as Dae and Young have shown us, but knowledge is forever."

At that moment Okami disappeared, and the Shinto Bridge appeared, shimmering before Paek. He crossed into the spirit world and taught many.

Power comes from needing little. The weight of greed sunk Dae in sand.

We must spend less when we are on unstable ground. Just as Dae was not strong enough to bear the weight of his greed on the sand, a side hustle is not stable enough to withstand the weight of huge expenses if you start using all the money you make.

There may come a point when your side hustle starts making money. You will be tempted to spend it on yourself. Do not do it. You are not rich yet. You need to know how to live modestly so you can put that money back into the company.

Always trade money for time or skill.

Money comes and goes, but time can never be recaptured. In addition, at the side hustle level, you are the asset. Accordingly, when you increase your skill, you are investing back into the asset.

As I went to war, I assembled weapons.

Want to know the great thing about making a little more money? You can buy better and better weapons for your army.

I believe I had an undiagnosed reading disorder as a child. I had to read something several times to comprehend it. Reading was a struggle, and I felt like I had to muscle through any kind of text. I always struggled

with standardized testing too—I scored well on the math sections, but
the reading comprehension? Forget about it.

Over the years I learned techniques that helped me read better—
not well, I still had to work at it, but well enough. Despite that (or
maybe because of it), I became obsessed with reading books, especially
books that would help me improve my skills. If you walked into my
office today, you'd see hundreds of books on my shelves, and I've read
them all.

Why am I telling you this? Well, I knew there was a chance that my
side hustle—now my full-time business—could fail. Even if I spent every
waking hour throwing all my energy into it, and even if I did everything
right, it could still not grow, and could eventually go under.

If it failed, I wanted to make sure there was an incredibly valuable
asset I could salvage.

That asset was me. I wanted to make sure that even if this business
failed, I would come out of it better—more resilient, more knowledge-
able, and better equipped for the next opportunity.

> You have to read and consume information
> relevant to your side hustle as if your business
> life depends on it, because it does.

I wanted to make sure that even if I lost this battle, I would still win
the war.

(By the way, with every venture I've been a part of since, I go in with
this same mindset: I identify the assets I will walk away with should the
venture fail. *Because ventures often do fail.*)

So I armed myself by investing in knowledge and in hiring people
to free up more time for my learning. For me and my specific business,
that meant learning more and more substantive areas of the law and

learning about innovative tech solutions that would help me deliver on my customer-centric goals.

It is here in my journey that I was able to expand beyond real estate closings. I made enough money to not only take classes and buy more books, but also attend seminars and pay people hourly to show me how to do things. I built strong relationships with these mentors.

You know what I needed to execute all this? Money. I needed money to invest back into myself. I did not buy a fancy car or expensive clothing. Those are depreciable assets that lose value when you buy them. I bought things that would stay with me forever and increase my value as an asset.

For my first couple of clients, I had my mentors do the work. They took all the money. I took zero, but I asked to shadow them and watch them do all the work at no extra cost. I would trade money for skill or time anytime. After a few dozen times, I knew enough to do these tasks on my own.

The thing that made me different from my competition was my perspective. Whereas my competitors were trained by other lawyers, my main coaches up to this point had been customers. I worked so closely with them that I was able to listen to the things that they loved and hated. Then I slowly worked to maintain what they loved and improve what they hated.

PRACTICE TIP

Reinvest Your Profits into Your Business

If you are lucky enough to discover a side hustle that is starting to make a profit, you have to be disciplined in the way you deploy your cash. Here is an approach to consider:

- **Step 1:** Set a budget for your business. You have to track your cash closely when you start—cash in and cash out. Come up with budgeted expenses. At the end of the month, look at your actual expenses. See if there is a difference. Over time your ability to forecast the costs should improve, and the difference should get smaller and smaller.

- **Step 2:** Do not overspend in your personal life. At the side hustle level, there is very little difference between you as an individual and your business. If you live wild and suck the life out of your side hustle by overspending on your personal life, your business won't last long.

- **Step 3:** Be very careful with outside money, such as bank loans or loans from family and friends, at the side hustle level. As a general rule I tell side hustlers not to take outside money. When you take money from people, they have power over you. And if you do this with the wrong party under the wrong terms, they can destroy your company. Put up your own money and then reinvest profits. Keep it simple. Stay in control. (If you are part of a start-up culture or investment group, that is different. Those businesses are built for outside money).

Please keep in mind that this is a complicated subject. The above advice is for side hustlers trying to break free from full-time employment.

CHAPTER 5 ENERGY

*The fifth step of the Tao of the side hustle is
to preserve your energy. Now that you have a
skill, an army, time, and treasure, you need to
maintain and grow all of these things. You can do
that successfully only if you also have energy.*

AFTER TIME, ENERGY IS THE MOST IMPORTANT CURRENCY
you have available to spend.

If you were about to run a marathon, you would train, eat well, get
plenty of sleep, and avoid drugs and alcohol, right?

Well, running a business is no different. And the race is a *lot* longer
and harder than a marathon. At some point you need to pull back on the
hustle and grind, and turn your attention to longevity.

I was so busy with work and my side hustle that I had to quit martial arts.
Not too long after this, my motion capture side hustle took another blow.

I experienced a pretty devastating injury. I had a full rupture in my left Achilles tendon that would require a twelve-month recovery. Game over.

This was devastating for me. But I was very lucky that I had flipped my motion capture side hustle into another side hustle that was much more lucrative.

When I was training under the monks at the Shaolin Temple, I used to make fun of the guys practicing tai chi. I thought those slow movements were boring and the whole thing looked goofy.

One of the monks tried to explain to me that tai chi means "the supreme martial art" because it focuses on health. But in my twenties, I was still too ignorant to really understand what he meant.

I'm glad that my coaches made me learn this art. The slow, soft movement helped prevent me from going crazy and really taught me the importance of taking care of myself. It was the only thing I could do as I was recovering.

Now that I'm a little older and everything cracks and hurts, I see how important energy and health are in prolonging time. You need health so that you can be sure to have the time you need for your business. In fact, you should approach your health as if you are waging a war that you cannot afford to lose.

There was once a great young warrior named Hanjun. He became great by always looking for ways to improve. He was a constant student of his craft, and as he grew stronger, he wanted to learn more and faster.

Hanjun heard of two wise monks living on Jeju Island who could help him with his training. The two monks, who were twins, named themselves the Sun and the Moon, and sometimes they could be a little confusing.

Hanjun decided to visit the monks. When he arrived he dropped to a knee and said, "I am Hanjun, and I want to learn to be the best at what I do. Can you help me?"

The twins smiled and looked at each other and started speaking.

The Sun said, "There is no such thing as being the best at what you do. Life is just a journey of improvement."

The Moon said, "Of course! You just must find your best self."

Hanjun, looking confused at the conflicting answers, said, "I am sorry, but I am confused."

The Sun said, "That is the purpose of your life: to work your way out of this confusion."

The Moon said, "There is no such thing as confusion, just the path to discovery."

This went on and on. Every time Hanjun opened his mouth, each monk gave a different answer. Hanjun could see what was happening. He slowed down the conversation to focus on something very specific.

Hanjun said, "I just want to know the best way to learn."

The Sun said, "Studying books."

The Moon said, "Go out and meet the people."

Hanjun pressed the twins. "Those are two different answers. Can each one of you explain?"

The Sun said, "Reading books gives you the wisdom of others in a shorter period of time."

The Moon said, "Books are past tense. You must meet people and know the world to understand present tense."

Hanjun said, "Well, which answer is better?"

Both the Sun and the Moon said at the same time, "Mine is."

Hanjun said, "You both can't be right."

The Sun said, "Which religion is the best?"

Hanjun stuttered, "I, I don't know. Wait, what does that have to do with anything? Look, you two are giving opposite answers all the time. It does not make any sense."

The Moon said, "Different religions are like people looking at the same painting from different angles. The angle will influence your perspective."

The Sun said, "So our answers are different but lead to the same place."

The Moon said, "Tree branches grow in many different directions, and the direction of a branch may influence the perspective of the bird that rests on it. However, if you trace the branches back far enough, you find they all have the same root."

The Sun and the Moon both said, "Life is all about perspective. Embrace your perspective while understanding the perspectives of others."

Hanjun said to himself, "So books and people are both the right answer. Books are written by people in the past tense. Meeting people helps you understand how we have evolved since the books were written. That is present tense. Understanding both allows you to see into the future tense."

The Sun and the Moon bowed, and Hanjun experienced a temporary enlightenment. Until the Sun threw a book at his head and said, "Stop thinking so much and go out and meet the people."

Our lives may take us in different directions, but ultimately we come back to the same root. We have to stay healthy to have the energy to experience this wonderful journey called life. You can study the world, but if you do not take care of yourself, you will not be able to experience it. Get out there and experience life!

I can't emphasize enough how important your own health is going to be as you launch and grow your business. It's the aspect of entrepreneurship that is too often ignored, or even dismissed, as side hustlers often take pride in how hard they are working or how many hours they are putting in, rather than considering the consequences of overextending themselves.

We learned at the beginning of this book that the following symbol, called bagua, represents Taoism. As noted earlier, *Tao* loosely translates to "the Path."

The Tao is all about the balance of the universe. Do you see the trigrams that surround the yin and yang symbol? Each trigram is strategically placed to represent a different energy and element.

There are many lessons we can draw from the bagua. In particular, we need balance in our lives to reach maximum performance. Balance of mind, body, and spirit.

There are three aspects to maintaining your health—physical, mental, and emotional and spiritual—and they are equally important.

PHYSICAL HEALTH

Energy comes from physical health, and the most important factor in physical fitness is what goes into your body. You must regulate what you eat and drink.

A wise man once told me that the key to wealth lies not in how much money you make, but in what you don't spend. Similarly, health is not how much you exercise, but what you do not eat.

This journey will be the most difficult of your life, and you need to be physically capable of taking it.

First, avoid drugs. Do not let them into your life. Drug use will eventually topple you. You'd be shocked at the number of successful people

I've known who lost their companies and their families through excessive use of drugs.

Second, try to avoid alcohol. If you do not drink, keep it that way. If you do, try everything you can to drink only in moderation.

I drink an occasional glass of wine at social events. But it's too easy for one drink to turn into too many. And alcohol abuse is tricky because it is easy to hide.

People are often tempted to use drugs and alcohol to unwind, to deal with stress and anxiety, or to come down from the adrenaline rush of a long day of work. Sometimes people believe they need to escape from reality. I get it, and was guilty of this myself. When I worked for a big firm, I dealt with stress by drinking alcohol and eating badly.

But your body doesn't need help in clearing out adrenaline (it does that on its own) nor do you need to escape reality (you're building a new, better reality, remember?). And drinking or using drugs doesn't actually alleviate stress. Using alcohol and drugs this way is simply a habit, one you are far better off not adopting in the first place.

One of my best friends had everything going for him. He had a successful business, a beautiful wife and kids, and a house in the suburb with the best school system.

He was also an alcoholic.

I didn't recognize the signs. I mean, I knew he liked a few drinks— but that's not a big deal, right? He was always so charming with his explanations.

It was not until he smashed his luxury car into a street median, drunk at ten o'clock in the morning, that I started to understand. Then he started making crazy business decisions that crushed his successful company. This then ripped his family apart. Unfortunately, in my line of work as a lawyer, I see this far too often. After seeing the effects of alcoholism firsthand, I worked hard to stop drinking altogether.

Third, avoid terrible, unhealthy foods. I stopped eating out some years ago because I want to know exactly what ingredients are in all my meals. Restaurants make money selling food, and some put ingredients into their recipes to encourage you to eat more and to spur cravings so you'll come back for more.

Take the time to make your own meals. Simple, modest meals from ingredients you can pronounce are better than much of what you'll buy prepackaged in stores or at restaurants.

MENTAL HEALTH

After you begin to regulate what goes into your body, turn your attention to your mental health.

We all have stress. The question is, How do we manage it?

The answer is not to numb ourselves or try to ignore what is causing the stress. Rather, the best way to manage our mental stress is to greet it head-on and deal with it.

There are three things I do to handle stress.

First, I rigorously limit my social media activity. Social media is an incredible tool, not just for staying connected with friends and learning about the world but for business development too. But too much social media is a bad thing. Spend time ingesting other types of information instead.

Read a book, travel, break bread with people. Reading allows you to learn both history and other people's perspectives. Travel builds self-confidence. Eating with others allows you to exchange ideas and open up to each other (online, we speak without consequence; in real life, our interactions must be filled with empathy).

Second, I try to live as simply as I can.

For my first job out of law school, I bought several fancy suits. It was stupid. I was stupid.

I thought those expensive suits would make people respect and like me more. All those suits did for me was chain me to my desk even more. They didn't impress anyone. Just the opposite: my clients probably thought their fees went to pay for my expensive fancy suits. They were right.

Stop buying things you don't need or things to impress others. Material things do not define you. Your character and actions define you. Nobody really cares what brands you wear or what kind of car you drive. They only care about whether you can make them feel better. And if you're a jerk, but a well-dressed jerk, they will see through you.

Instead, live as basic a lifestyle as you can manage. I still dress professionally, but not to impress anyone with a brand. You can be both professional and basic.

Third, I get rid of the toxic people in my life.

My company has a strict policy: no jerks or mean people. If you disrespect a client or someone on my staff, I ask you to leave.

> Create self-respect boundaries and
> enforce them.

People think this is crazy, because it sometimes means giving up a client relationship and revenue. But to me, it's actually part of our brand. And I don't want or need mean customers stressing out my team, because my team members will carry that stress with them for far longer than the nasty interaction. No, if a customer cannot be professional and respectful, we don't need their money.

If someone is making you miserable, tell them. If they are unwilling to reflect and change, then get them out of your world. If you can't get them out of your world completely, then find a way to set strong boundaries.

EMOTIONAL AND SPIRITUAL HEALTH

With a fit body and a less stressed mind, we can turn to the third aspect of health.

The Japanese word *satori*, in a Buddhist context, loosely translates to "enlightened." My interpretation of the word is self-discovery. My own journey toward enlightenment began only when I connected my physical and mental selves to my emotional and spiritual sides.

We're only here on earth for a short time. So make this life worth living. When you are laying on your death bed, will you think back about the extra projects you took on? Probably not. In my profession as a lawyer, I have seen many people near the end of their lives. In my experience, most think about loved ones and cherished memories.

You will probably think about the things most important to your life. Reflect on what those are and prioritize them.

I think one reason people like to do business with me and my company is that when they do, they become part of our community. I want them to know my kids, and I want to know theirs. Connect more deeply with people, and not only will it be good for your business, but it will be good for you emotionally.

As the warrior learned in the story at the beginning of this chapter, wherever we are, if we all go back, we all have the same roots. In addition, we all have the same destination. Just as tree branches eventually fall to the ground, so shall we return to the earth.

PRACTICE TIP

Calm as the Ocean

Meditation is a complicated subject, but I am going to show you one of my go-to approaches. The technique I use is practical and one that you can do every day. Meditation is really important in martial arts because it enhances mental clarity and focus. This same technique works in business too.

Meditation helps you slow things down and give your racing mind a break. The breathing is an exercise in focus; its purpose is to help you find the things that are important.

The reason I am showing you my meditation technique is that I do not find many of the meditation practices out there practical. What follows is a technique taught to me by some very high-level martial arts monks.

My own path involves daily meditation. Meditation is how I align myself, how I connect body, mind, emotion, and spirit on a daily basis. This approach should take you no more than five minutes. Do the following:

Step 1: Put on some relaxing music and dim the lights.

Step 2: Sit down in a comfortable position (preferably with your legs crossed) and close your eyes. Take five deep breaths.

Step 3: Begin with your body and focus momentarily on each of the five senses (taste, touch, sight, sound, smell).

Step 4: Then turn your attention to your mind by focusing on a challenging moment in your past. Clarify how you will better face similar challenges in the future. Do not dwell on the past or the future for too long, but do give them some thought. Take some deep breaths, and slowly bring yourself back to the present. Be conscious of your inhale and exhale.

Step 5: Turn your attention to your emotions by opening up your chakras (the energy points in your body). Start at the base of your spine and move up to the crown of your head. You can move through the statements in the steps below either in your mind or by saying them out loud.

1. **Earth:** In your mind's eye, start with your focus at your root, located at the base of your spine. Say to yourself, "I am safe and secure."
2. **Water:** In your mind's eye, move up to your tailbone. Say to yourself, "I can adapt to anything. I am creative."
3. **Boundary:** In your mind's eye, move up to your solar plexus. Say to yourself, "I know my boundaries; they define who I am. I will defend my boundaries."

4. **Fire:** In your mind's eye, move up to your heart. Say to yourself, "I am loved and know how to love. I belong to a tribe."

5. **Air:** In your mind's eye, move up to your throat. Say to yourself, "My words have power. I will be cautious about what I say to others."

6. **Third eye:** In your mind's eye, move up to your "third eye" in the forehead area. Say to yourself, "I will start to look at what is in front of me."

7. **Crown:** In your mind's eye, move to the top of your head and reach *satori*. Say to yourself, "I have no control. I must let it go." You cannot control the universe; you can only ride the waves. Learn to let go and appreciate. That is enlightenment.

We're taking baby steps here. Many of us have a lot going on. But all of us can put aside five minutes a day.

PART 2

STABILIZE

THE TAO OF THE SIDE HUSTLE IS A PATH FROM SALARY TO profit. This can be a difficult journey because, for many, the distance between salary and profit is huge.

This book is itemizing the steps of your Tao to get this. Those first five steps are the basic anchor values you will need to get started. Never lose those, because as you grow and your business adapts, you will constantly need to balance those same five values.

When you make it this far, it probably means that one of your side hustles started working. Now we want to transition it from a side hustle to a sustainable operation. Please note that you need to be selective on the side hustle you choose to stabilize, as not all side hustles are intended to grow.

☯

So my side hustle started making a little money. I was cranking out real estate closings and rapidly learning other closely related areas of the law. I quit my full-time day job and stopped taking on martial arts motion capture projects. I was completely focused on my law firm. Technology was beginning to catch up. Vendors began offering lessons and I was consuming massive amounts of information nonstop.

Translated to the lessons of part 1, I identified my skill, began to build my army, deployed my treasure, and started to buy back time and energy.

I was by no means wealthy, but I was making enough that I was able to quit my job. I was now a small business owner.

Well, now what? I had no idea what I was supposed to do next.

I was personally cool with that. I even started coasting just a little—I'd even occasionally do yoga during the day. Most importantly, I felt in control of the business, and without my day job, my life was relatively stress-free.

My wife was still working full-time at a job she hated, pulling insane hours. Coming home super relaxed and happy while my wife had had a brutal day was less than optimal. But still, I was having a blast.

Until one night at dinner when she shared the most amazing news: "Don, we are pregnant!"

If you're a parent, you probably know what happened next. As excited as I was, the next day I woke up thinking, "I really need to step up my game."

I was about to grow up, and fast.

I was super excited. I'd always wanted kids. But I knew that kids would change everything. Kids are really expensive.

Spiritually, I practice Buddhism, and I strongly believe that the gift of life is priceless. Accordingly, I knew I owed my wife a lot for the gift of children. Plus, she had stood by me when I was broke! I immediately knew that I was going to have to grow the business big enough so that she could quit her job too.

Doing so was easier said than done.

At this point, even though things seemed to be going well, my revenue was unstable and unpredictable. A lot of revenue would come in all at once, then there would be none for long stretches. I needed to figure out how to even out the revenue stream over the entire year and how to support costs during both up and down months.

Part 1 was about your basics. Basics are really important. They are the building blocks to continue your growth. And they are there when you face adversity.

But now I was past the basics. I needed to graduate to the next level of my life and stabilize the business so that my wife could join me.

This is the part of the movie where I made it out of the rigorous training and I was ready to test my ability against some of the smaller bad guys.

Again, I turned to my martial arts background for answers.

In martial arts, after you win a few battles, you may become champion—but then everyone else will be gunning for you. You need new strategies after you've tasted success.

We are about to move into part 2 of this book. When you get this far, that means one of your side hustles has shown some promise to evolve into a small business.

The purpose of a business is to profit.

(That is not to say that you need to profit at all costs. This book promotes balancing making a profit with exercising social responsibility, as taught through Tao and Buddhism, but this is a business book. Without profit, your business will not last long.)

This next stage of the book will discuss stabilizing your side hustle into a small business. Stabilizing your position in battle can be broken down into five concepts: armory, battlefield, new weapons, fortification, and combat.

Part 2 guides you in stabilizing your side hustle in these five areas. We will continue our Tao here. Let's start walking.

CHAPTER 6 ☯ ARMORY

*The first step toward stabilization on the Tao
of the side hustle is to get control of the rations
and manage the resources in your armory.*

GOING TO WAR IS SO MUCH MORE THAN COMBAT. YOU MUST learn to manage your resources. If your troops cannot replenish their supplies, they will fail. If you overconsume your supplies at the beginning of the campaign, your army will not sustain itself.

Soldiers cannot march and carry out orders on empty stomachs.

Many wars have been won and lost by cutting off the enemy's supplies. If your opponent cannot feed its troops, it will not be able to fight for long. If you cannot feed your own troops, it is *your* army that will fail.

When I quit my full-time job and became a full-time employee of my business, the single most important thing I did was cut my personal expenses. As many of you know, this is really hard with a new baby.

Similarly, if you run through your company's resources, you will suck the life out of your company before it can take off. You have to nurture your company. To avoid overconsumption, you have to ensure you are living "lean" in both your personal and professional life. Spend only within your budget. This will allow you to reinvest in your company—in other words, to replenish its resources—and sustain it.

A side hustle needs cash flow to live. Most side hustlers do not have a ton of disposable income to deploy, so most cash flow will need to come from profit.

The income from my side hustle—as with most at this stage—was feast or famine. You need to save your profits from the good months and have low overhead to handle the inevitable slow months or downturns in the economy.

> Volume may cure all sins, but living below your means is the shortest route to heaven.

I know how tempting it is to show off your spoils with fancy cars, jewelry, and clothes. The problem is that if your company needs a capital call (a cash infusion from the owner) and you've spent all the money, then you have to cut back on provisions for members of your army, whether employees, business partners, or independent contractors.

Cash flow motivates movement and velocity from all these parties. If you stop paying people or your payments to them start becoming very slow, the performance from those around you will decrease dramatically.

A way to nurture cash flow is by keeping expenses low.

According to the Buddhist tradition, the gods decided that once a person gains enlightenment, they move into heaven. Each person who fails to reach enlightenment during their lifetime is reincarnated—and continues to be reincarnated until enlightenment is achieved.

Just before souls are reincarnated and returned to the human world, they must drink *ijda* tea, which makes them forget their prior lives. This keeps the game fair; each person starts from scratch in the search for enlightenment.

There once was a soul who served a time in hell and was about to be reincarnated. The dragon spirit diluted the *ijda* tea, replacing half with water.

Yama, the lord of the underworld, saw the trick and sensed that the dragon spirit was floating around. Yama tried to stop the soul from drinking the diluted potion, but it was too late: Ryu was born.

The episode haunted Yama. He wanted the soul of Ryu back.

Ryu was born into poverty. He knew only a hard life. But Ryu also had a sixth sense—he was able to see into the future, including the old age and death of all those he met. This vision made Ryu kind to all, and he would often perform manual labor to help those around him whose fates he could see.

Ryu's kindnesses frustrated Yama beyond belief! One day, Yama reached his limit. He transformed himself into a human king, clothed head to toe in luxurious fur.

Yama approached Ryu, showing him gold. "Young man, come here," Yama said. "I can give you any riches your heart desires and make any wish come true. All you have to do is follow me."

But Ryu thought of all the visions he'd seen of people taking their last breath. Not one had thought of their money. He responded, "I am sorry, your majesty. I have seen true wealth. It does not come from gold."

Yama said, "Then tell me what you want. Diamonds? Cash? I can give you anything."

Ryu thought for a moment. "True wealth does not come from gold or diamonds," he said. "True wealth comes from realizing that you do not need those diamonds and that those diamonds have only the value you give them. True wealth is happiness."

Yama immediately transformed into the devil and was sucked back into the underworld. Ryu had achieved enlightenment, and his soul would not return to the underworld.

To move forward, you must try to walk with the lightest load possible. This way, you will be prepared to traverse life's ups and downs.

Luxury items are nice, but you do not need them. In fact, the wealthiest people I know do their best to show off as little as possible.

As I transitioned from my full-time job into a full-time employee of my side hustle, I made all kinds of mistakes. What allowed my business to survive? I kept my expenses super low. I bootstrapped everything.

The Japanese word *fudoshin* means "immovable mind"—it's basically a fancy way of saying "discipline." When your side hustle starts making money, you need self-discipline to avoid going out and spending on stupid things. You have to rely on your *fudoshin*.

I was bringing employees on and wanted to bring my wife into the business full-time, so I knew that I needed to be able to make payroll—including paying *her*—in good months and bad.

CUT EXPENSES TO THE BONE

You must cut your personal expenses down to the bone. So much depends on you when you have a side hustle or are starting a small business. The number one reason I see small businesses go under? Cash flow problems.

I cut out every expense I possibly could. I moved my family to the house I was born in (we happen to still live in it to this day), I bought a used car (which I happen to still drive to this day!), and I cut out alcohol—it's crazy how much we spend on that.

I was experiencing some success, but I still bought my suits on eBay. I recall once winning an award and pulling up to the ceremony in my beat-up old car with infant seats in the back. Business colleagues and competitors laughed at me; I remember one of them saying, "The car reflects the driver."

I thought, "That's the stupidest thing I've ever heard. My car gets me from point A to point B, and that's all I ask it to do. I prefer to have my company reflect my character."

Every time the economy around my business has fluctuated, due to worldwide crashes or local competition or technology disruptions, I have seen competitors cut wages and cut staff. I've never done either.

You know who takes the pay cut? Me. I get paid less. Never my team. Your employees eat first. You eat last, and only what is left over.

After my wife had our first daughter, she did in fact join the company. My personal expenses were so low that I was able to pay her a full-time salary. Even when my revenues went down 40 percent in a given month, she and the rest of the team were paid.

You know who didn't get paid? Me. But that is the risk of being a business owner. If there is no profit, you do not eat.

We had competitors who lived in million-dollar mansions and drove Porsches, but who had to lay off people every time the market went down. But markets are cyclical—they will always go down eventually! Every business has its seasons. Why do business owners react as if this is a surprise and take it out on their employees?

Eventually I understood that these competitors were opposing armies that had failed to replenish their supplies, had cut their own supply lines, and were certain to starve their own troops. My competitors' lack of foresight allowed me and my army to win our battles.

You must stay ready for winter. Take your ego out of it, and get rid of the things you do not need or the things you are buying just for appearances. Pour your cash into the asset you are building, which in turn will produce more cash for you.

MANAGE YOUR DEBT

I do not believe side hustlers should take on outside money in the form of investors or debt. These quickly become a burden—financially, emotionally, operationally—and thus are generally way too expensive. Use your own sweat and money to get the momentum going. Then use profits to grow. If your company cannot make a profit—even a small one—maybe it's not the best idea.

Once your cash flow can consistently support the weight of the business, a responsible level of debt (if done right) can really help you, but not at this point for most side hustlers.

I recognize that some kinds of businesses do need substantial investment just to get off the ground. In some circumstances, debt is the only way to start or scale your business, and in those cases, I love using it. However, side hustles are not these kinds of businesses.

Here's my point: when misused, debt can be a form of imprisonment. It can be a trap, and a trap that is very hard to get out of. Remember what happened to me with my student debt.

> **Live lean so your company can eat.**

There are two types of debt you'll likely consider at various times: personal debt and business debt.

Personal Debt

You are directly connected to your small business financially. If the owner of a small business has huge expenses and personal debts, the owner will be tempted to suck the business dry of any available profits to cover those personal expenses rather than investing the profits back into the business.

In the United States we are taught to take on enormous debt to finance our lives. Most of us amass huge student loans. Then we take out as large a mortgage as we can for our personal residence—usually at our credit limit—which we then will have to pay off over thirty years.

And then we start a family, so the cycle can begin all over again with our children's debts. It's a vicious cycle of debt, and it's really hard to break.

It's nuts!

And the cost of that American Dream of education, homeownership, and family is completely different today from what our baby boomer relatives experienced. The debt we are experiencing is often a multiple of that taken on by our parents or grandparents.

I know it's hard. But to the extent you possibly can, try to defer as much personal debt as you can until your business begins to scale. If you can't defer everything, defer as much as you can and stay as lean as possible.

I've mentioned my own student loan debt, which is not dischargeable in bankruptcy. How did I get out from underneath that huge load?

My strategy consisted of paying down one painful dollar at a time. I would pay down the smallest debts first. When that debt was paid down, then I redeployed that money plus the freed-up money to the next-largest debt. I kept repeating this painful process. Over time the process began to snowball. It took me nearly twelve years after graduating law school, but I was finally able to get my debts under control.

Business Debt

As I mentioned before, business debt can be very useful—but be careful that you are taking it on strategically and that you are taking on as little as you actually need for a specific purpose.

The huge risk with any business debt is that you are creating a new sunk cost—a hole that must be filled each month. Be careful that you can cover that cost without having to resort to more borrowing, or cutting staff, or reducing marketing spend, or anything else that will slow growth.

If your company has strong cash flow, then leveraging debt can be a powerful tool. What's the best way to use it? To improve the asset (your business) in order to generate even more cash flow.

Yes, your business is an asset. It generates revenue. Just like investment real estate is an asset—it generates revenue. Reasonable debt against cash-flowing assets that improves the assets and generates even more revenue is not inherently bad. When you've reached this point with your business, you can preserve your cash to invest in other things while using debt to grow the revenue-generating assets.

MAKE INFORMED DECISIONS

In my business, I help my customers make the best decisions they can. I'm there to warn of potential risks and pitfalls and to provide great information. People want control, or at least the illusion of control. They want to be able to choose for themselves what to do. So I have to provide great information and advice in order to create the most informed customer.

This power I give to my clients is the same I need to give myself in running my business. You must be appropriately informed to make good choices. You have to track the money going in and out.

Let me tell you a true horror story of mine. When I was getting started with my small business, I did not have a ton of checks to write, as I was mostly set up on autopay. However, I did have to write a few checks every month. Well, it turns out there are criminals who deliberately target United States mailboxes. They steal checks out of the mailbox, change the name of the payee to their own, and deposit them into their own fake accounts (apparently, people can set up fake bank accounts online without ever going into a branch). Unfortunately, someone did this to one of my checks and stole the money out of my account. This happens a lot, as evidenced by the long lines at the bank dealing with this issue.

Of course, the person who was supposed to get the check still wanted their money. I had to pay that person again, so I lost twice. My bank's fraud prevention states that you have to report this sort of issue in thirty days, or you lose the money. Thank the universe that I do a bank reconciliation at the end of each month checking each cleared check. I caught the stolen check and got my money back.

You must track every dollar in and out, and have current reports about your business, so you can make informed decisions.

> **The only way to make informed decisions is with accurate data.**

Friends and enemies will lie; numbers do not. You need data to make sure the end results are the right results—a reflection of the inputs you and your team have put into play.

Forget ROI, EPS, ARR, IRR, or whatever acronym you throw at me. At the side hustle level, the most important thing to track is cash. Use a monthly cash receipts and cash disbursements journal that simply tracks the cash going in and the cash going out. Just tracking cash month to month will help you see trends and spot storm clouds on the horizon.

You need to create and maintain these reports yourself. I believe it's really difficult to be a passive owner of a business and have any kind of success. You can hire people to take things off your plate, but basic reports, like those tracking cash receipts and disbursements, are not something you should delegate. You need to pay attention and make sure things are running exactly as you want.

REINVEST IN YOUR ARMY

If your teammates become very skilled and successful, competitors will try to take them. You spent all this time, energy, and money to train someone, and then *bam*—some vulture swoops down offering a 7 percent raise and recruits them away from your team. Not only do you experience downtime from losing that person, but you have to start the hiring and training processes all over again.

Invest by paying your staff so generously that they will not leave—because you can't afford turnover.

My first golden rule is to treat others the way I want to be treated. My second golden rule is to make sure that everyone at the dinner table not only eats but wins. I want the people around me to win, and win big.

My team works really hard. I expect that, they know I expect it, and they expect it of me and each other. I would put my team up against anyone's in competition.

You should be able to say the same about your team. And so, be generous to them. Gone are the days when only the people in the C-suite and passive investors took all the earnings. Employees today—especially millennial and Gen Z employees—are too smart and savvy to accept that (good for them). To keep top-notch talent, you will need to pay your team well.

I never cease to be amazed when I hear other business leaders complain about turnover and difficulty in hiring. Inevitably, I ask how much they are offering their employees, and about incentives. Sometimes the answer is a salary that's barely above minimum wage (and I operate in Chicago, a relatively expensive place to live). The executives would not be able to live on that salary, so how can they expect someone else to? You cannot set up your business so that you are the only one who wins.

In addition to paying your employees well as soon as they come in the door, incentivize them for truly great performance. Signal that while they will be well taken care of for doing the job competently, they can earn even more by reaching certain clearly understandable objectives. You'll be amazed at how your team will respond.

Invest in an army that reflects the world.

Diversity leadership is good business. If you want to capture emerging markets, you have to be able to genuinely connect with them. Don't merely market to women or minorities—develop women and minorities as leaders at the top of your organization, with true decision-making authority. These leaders will connect to markets better than any advertising or marketing activities ever will.

Many customers view companies as part of a community with social responsibilities. Customers are demanding transparency of leadership. You should be mindful of your leadership team.

> Here is a challenge: take a picture of your leadership team. If the picture completely lacks diversity, you should be mindful that customers will hold you accountable both with their purchasing power and in the court of public opinion.

Invest in the armies that surround, support, and sustain you.

Create an ecosystem of generosity, appreciation, and loyalty. What do I mean by that?

When you succeed, spread opportunities and love around you. If you become known as a giver, people will want to do business with you and be around you. If you are known as a greedy, stingy type, no one will forget that, and no one will want to do business with you, hang around you, or work for you longer than they have to. Just as taking profits out of the company may spike your income in the short term, pinching pennies may help your short-term profitability, but over the long haul it's both bad for your brand and bad for your business.

Look for chances to be generous beyond your day-to-day world. For example, as my business grew and I was in a better position financially, I returned to the neighborhood where I'd grown up to see how I could reinvest in it. My old 'hood didn't need people giving advice or inspiration. The people needed jobs. So I started seeking out and hiring people from the neighborhood, which in turn helped fuel the local economy.

That mindset of generosity extends to business deals and conflict. In a business deal, I try to work things out so that everyone walks away with a clear path to their own success. I see it as part of my job as your partner in the deal to make sure you are successful—which in turn will give you a vested interest in maintaining and growing the deal. Contracts are great, but if your business partner is getting screwed, best of luck to you in enforcing the agreement. Business litigation rarely leads to growth and profitability.

In a conflict, I try to work things out so that everyone walks away with their honor intact. In any good settlement, nobody walks away truly happy, with everything they demanded, but all walk away feeling their honor and integrity are intact. The only way this happens is if you enter the process of resolving the conflict with a highly intentional sense of generosity.

PRACTICE TIP

Money in the Bank

When you start your side hustle, your goal may be to make a couple of extra dollars to make ends meet. You may find along your journey (as I did) that some side hustles will not work. Maybe it's a bad idea, the timing is bad, or the market conditions are wrong, but some side hustles are just not going to work.

However, if you find that one of your side hustles does work and you think it can morph into a small business, you cannot suck the profits out of it. Do not take your profits and blow them on stupid stuff! You must reinvest it back into the company.

You do not need a nicer car. You need better tools to serve the needs of your customers. Your customers do not really care if you have a really nice car; they care if you are solving their problems the way they want.

Here are some specific steps I recommend:

Step 1: Get rid of all unnecessary expenses. Cars and watches do not define you. Your character defines you. If you need fancy stuff to support your ego, you have self-confidence issues that you need to reconcile. At this point in the life of your side hustle, your business needs the money, not you.

Step 2: Budget all necessary expenses. You inevitably need money to live. Trust me, I know the pain of the costs of balancing groceries, diapers, health care, and day care. I have been there. But when you have a budget, you set a number and stick to it. If fancy coffees break your budget, you had better downgrade to instant.

Step 3: Reinvest profits back into the business. Take all disposable income and put it back into making a better mousetrap. The customer does not care that you are short on money for groceries or that you want to spend more time with your kids. The customer has their own problems. At the end of the day, the only thing the customer cares about is how you are going to make their life easier or better. Period, end of story.

Let's say you have an interest in starting a side hustle fixing up old houses and selling them. How does the above translate into this kind of hustle?

- First, build a skill that is relevant. For example, become a home inspector so you can spot potential problems with a home. Or become a real estate agent so you know the before-and-after values of a home. Or become a contractor so you know the relative costs, time requirements, and values of the potential repairs.

- Take the money you make from that job to identify tools to improve the experience of the customer. For example, I know a contractor whose business model is using his own construction team on his flips. This way he is in charge of quality control and costs.
- If the customer is getting a better product or experience at a better price from you than from a competitor, they will refer friends and keep coming back.

The contractor I referred to above pours all his resources back into his flips. Because he is in charge of quality control and costs, he can provide a high-quality product at a low cost. People keep coming back and buying from him.

After a decade, his side hustle of flipping homes makes more than his contracting business. You would never know this from the fifteen-year-old car he drives.

CHAPTER 7 ☯ BATTLEFIELD

*The second step toward stabilization on
the Tao of the side hustle is to understand
the conditions of your battlefield.*

YOU WOULDN'T USE FOOTBALL CLEATS ON A FROZEN hockey rink. And you wouldn't lace up skates to go play basketball.

Rather, you need to understand the rules of the environment you intend to play in, make sure you're using the right tools, and watch closely to see if new or different tools are needed.

When I was competing in martial arts, I understood the surface, the dimensions of the ring, the weapons my opponent and I were to use—and how all these things might change during the course of our battle.

As a businessperson, I never thought of myself as a particularly impressive business thinker. But I do believe I am a pretty good predictor of the weather.

What does any of this mean? This chapter will explain how to understand the battlefield, how to read the conditions, and how to think about the flow of battle across the terrain.

There once was a young warrior at the top of her class, the best performer in all aspects of martial arts, who could quickly subdue anyone who dared challenge her. She was so good, she began to run out of challengers.

One day she approached her teacher and asked, "*Sifu*, I have run out of opponents in my class. May I go to other schools to find new challengers?" (In martial arts culture, *sifu* loosely means "teacher," but also "father/mother figure"—someone with a deep vested interest in a person's development.)

The old monk smiled. "I am so proud of your development. You have beaten everyone . . . except for one person. That person is your equal in power, talent, and hard work."

"Who?" asked the young warrior. "I would like to challenge them immediately!"

The old monk nodded and said, "I will show you." Then he walked his young student to a koi fishpond. The old monk asked the young warrior to look at the pond and admire the fish. "This temple has been in our clan for generations, and we continue to survive to this day through our ability to adapt to change and grow as a community," the old monk said. "Your next challenger is right there." He pointed to the water.

The young warrior was confused. "The koi?" she asked.

"No," said the monk. "Look closer . . . at the challenger staring back at you."

The young warrior suddenly realized she was looking at her reflection in the water. This confused her very much.

The old monk, seeing the confusion in her eyes, said, "Any person can be a king or a queen, but only a great leader can create an empire. You must challenge yourself and make those around you as good as you. I challenge you to make your classmates as good as you, and work in unison—to go from one strong finger to a powerful fist."

The young warrior understood. She and the monk agreed that she would teach her classmates.

But as the young warrior began to train them, she quickly became frustrated. All the other students had different abilities and skill levels. They could not do what she could do and couldn't even do what she asked.

After a few days of this, she again approached the old monk. "*Sifu*, the students are . . . not good. Some are too fast, and some are too slow. Some don't know what they are doing, and some don't care. They just are not as good as I am. What should I do?"

The old monk replied, "I see that you are already losing to yourself, my pupil."

The young warrior was shocked, and even more confused. The other students were at fault, surely. How could it be that *she* was losing?

The old monk said, "Do you know the difference between chess and checkers? Checkers pieces are all the same and move in the same way. But chess pieces are unique: each piece moves in its own way. In chess, if you do not understand how each piece moves or how to position it, then you cannot play. And if you cannot position and move the pieces properly, it's not their fault—it's your fault!"

The young warrior understood. She sat down and began thinking about each of her classmates—their strengths and their weaknesses. She then began training each one accordingly, amplifying each person's strengths and eliminating their weaknesses.

After some time, as a unit, her students became more powerful than she was. Once again, she approached her teacher, the old monk. "*Sifu*," she said, "I have taught my team to be stronger and better than I could ever be."

The old monk replied, "Yes, my young pupil. You are now playing chess."

Life and business are all about preparing and positioning. Position your teammates for success.

Life is a pickup game and you need to play with what you've got. We all want to work with the best teammates in fair weather, but life does not work that way. With the right positioning, you can at least get the best out of your team regardless of the conditions.

As your business grows, conditions will continue to evolve. There are many different battlefield conditions for you to understand and master, but in the case of side hustles I believe understanding these three is the most important: emerging markets, business cycles, and upstream versus downstream. All three of these conditions create massive changes, which open up opportunities for nimble side hustlers.

BATTLEFIELD #1: EMERGING MARKETS

The first critical question is this: Is your business in an emerging, mature, or dying market? Think of the answer to this question as being like your location on a GPS map.

Let's start with an example that most families can relate to: playing games.

Back in the day, families used to play board games for entertainment. Board games were a mature market, with steady sales from established game companies.

Then video games, a huge emerging market, overtook board games. Eventually, "gaming" was synonymous with video games, and board games—while still manufactured and sold—were a revenue rounding error relative to the revenue from video games.

This played out in a series of phases.

Phase 1: When video games first launched, they were in an emerging market—and one with high barriers to entry. Video games were first produced in large cabinets, which could be found only in public arcades. (I remember spending my whole allowance in an arcade. I loved these games.) Both the cabinet-style games and the arcades were hard to scale—they were too expensive, too inconvenient, and just too big for home use.

Phase 2: Next, the video game arcade market became a mature market (with waning innovation) and the new emerging market became the home console market. The early game systems plugged into your television, and the games were distributed through cartridges. These game systems were easy to scale, and the market was literally every household with a television. New revenue streams were created with each new game release.

Phase 3: Next, the video game cartridge/disc market became the mature market, and downloads became the new emerging market. Improvements to the game systems allowed downloadable games, which replaced cartridges. The game system itself stored and updated all the games, eliminating the need to deal with defective cartridges or discs and the need to store games. Companies eliminated distribution costs and increased profits.

Do you see how the emergence of the video game market was actually a *series* of changes to the market, each of which effectively destroyed the prior mature market? If you were in the video game industry, you needed to move fast and accurately predict the change in consumer behavior and demand (as well as the technological innovations of your competitors). The entire market went from popping tokens into arcade consoles to downloading and playing games over Wi-Fi at home in a relatively short amount of time. You might have been dominant in the arcade market—and reduced to nothing just a few years later.

In the context of martial arts and Buddhism, the Japanese word *muso* means "formlessness."

It means you have no form in combat. Your form changes based on the facts and circumstances of your situation. Your form leverages the terrain to best achieve victory in your conflict. For example, if the fight is standing and you are at a distance, you kick or punch. If the fight gets close, you move to the clinch and use your elbows and knees. If the fight gets to the ground, you wrestle and grapple. (For my Chinese friends, the analogy is *changquan*—"Long Fist"—if you are at a distance and *Chen taijiquan*—"Chen tai chi"—if you are close.)

Complete formlessness. It matters not where you are. You adapt. Adaptability always trumps strength, knowledge, and speed. Strength, knowledge, and speed are relative to your environment but change the environment. The nimble and adaptive thrive.

Think you are smarter than everyone because you have some knowledge? Look at real estate. Remember when real estate agents controlled knowledge of pricing through access to the multiple listing service (MLS)? Now a consumer can get that information (subject to some variability) online.

Real estate agents still provide extremely important value propositions, but the knowledge power is now in the hands of the consumer.

Value proposition simply refers to the reasons why a customer should hire you. Value is the thing you offer a person to give you money in exchange. To sustainably receive money from customers, the value you offer should solve a problem.

People work hard for their money. Your solution needs to be compelling enough that your customers would consistently decline doing it themselves and pay you to do it instead. In addition, customer's needs evolve, so your value must too.

Formlessness. Adaptability.

There are many video game arcades lying dead in the graveyard due to lack of *muso*.

How do you achieve formlessness? How do you become adaptable? Get down to your core value proposition and imagine the ways your customers will want to consume your service five years from now. Put yourself in their shoes. Your business is about their journey, not yours.

You probably aren't in the market of selling games. What market *are* you in? And do you think it's emerging, mature, or dying?

If you think you are in an emerging market, take advantage of your position, but do not get complacent. Just as the seasons change, so will consumer behavior.

Many side hustles start in a mature market. Businesses in mature markets are easier to replicate because the blueprints of the other businesses are out there. It is easier to slide in.

If you think you are in a mature market, your competition is likely differentiating themselves by cutting prices for the customer. Players in a mature market tend to focus on operational efficiencies to cut costs. If you are in a mature market fighting over pricing, you will probably need to have very strong systems and processes, and make your money on volume. And you'll want to be on the lookout for an exit strategy to move yourself into the next emerging market.

You'll need to be ready for anomalies too.

For example, my side hustle worked in part because I entered a mature market and the majority of the incumbents did not adapt or innovate quickly enough. Technology was pushing for a faster velocity and many of the service providers struggled to keep up with that.

Online retail companies were offering quicker and cheaper ways to purchase. *Oh, you like this coat? Click here and put it in your cart. Give us payment, tell us where to ship it, and there's no need to sit in traffic. Oh, by the way, here is a discount since you bought online.*

That seamless customer experience carried over into every part of the customer's life. They demanded the same set of frictionless service.

The incumbents had entered what they perceived as a "pull business"— that is, a business with proprietary technology or a special skill that "pulls" customers in. (As opposed to a "push business," which requires marketing to "push" to sell a commodity product.) These incumbents possessed special knowledge and used it to control the market.

However, the internet eliminated their special skill and knowledge; within an extremely short amount of time, the services the incumbents offered became commodity, rather than specialized, services. At the same time, the internet enabled a wave of vendors, and coincidentally law schools dramatically increased the number of new graduates.

At my company, we always try to be early adopters of technology that improves the customer experience. Things that really worked very early on were virtual document review and e-signatures. The virtual document review allowed us to screen share and walk the customer through complicated documents line by line. Then, after they approved the document, the e-signature process allowed us to simply send over a signature request to finish things up.

Please note that both of these services saved the customer time. Remember when I said you will always be trading the assets itemized in the first five chapters? As your business evolves, you will need new solutions, and you can use those five assets as guidance to evaluate your customer's needs.

Customers at that time demanded a faster pace. If service providers did not respond to them in less than twenty-four hours, the customers would get angry.

The old lawyers could no longer compete, because their assembly lines could not meet the new consumer demands for speed. They knew things were different, but they didn't understand *how* the market had shifted so fast, and so they had no idea what was needed to adapt. This is a huge advantage for side hustlers, because we are nimble. We can adapt quicker.

The law firms had never needed to innovate before; they failed to innovate now. I'm writing this in 2022, and I still deal with some of the remaining longtime incumbents who use a *fax machine* all day long!

I knew I was entering a mature market. But mature markets often have opportunities for adaptable companies. Like the phoenix rising from the ashes, mature dying markets often give birth to new markets (as the video game example above shows us). If you time it right, you can usher in new eras from video game cabinets, to cartridges, to downloads.

Rather than build my company around the old special skills model, I built it around the customer needs and process innovation of the next era. I needed to be patient. It did not happen overnight, but when the change did eventually happen, I was ready. The old guard may not have been able to keep up with the velocity of change; we built our business around it.

If you are in a maturing market, the important question to ask yourself is, Where are the emerging markets, and how can your business transition to the first position in one of them? Where do you see changes in customer expectations, technological efficiency, disruptive models, and so on that would lead you to believe that an emerging market will soon swallow your mature market—and how do you put your own business squarely in the mix?

Timing is everything. Technology moves fast, but consumer behavior lags behind, and it can take decades for mass adoption. You may still have a viable, profitable business for years after the moment you understand your mature market is dying! But the great thing about analyzing your business in these terms is that it gives you the opportunity to both capture the remaining profit from the mature market *and* be first past the post in the emerging market.

BATTLEFIELD #2: BUSINESS CYCLES (BULL AND BEAR)

The second battlefield characteristic is the business cycle.

Think of this as knowing what season you are in, so you can anticipate the weather. You don't want to be caught wearing board shorts in the middle of winter.

Most businesses operate in cycles. The first cycle is the annual cycle. For example, retail businesses typically build their annual cycle around the holiday season, including the clearance season immediately after the October to Christmas Eve rush. (The reason that many retail companies have a fiscal year ending January 31 rather than the end of the calendar year is to include all those extra post-Christmas sales.)

Another cycle is the overall economy. A bull market occurs when the economy is growing and individual businesses are fueled by that growth. A bear market occurs when things slow down. Both types of economy will affect your business.

Some businesses thrive only in one economy or the other. But the economy will always go up and down—so you really want a business that will do well in both bull and bear markets.

> The biggest mistake people make in business is that when times are good, they think it's because they are amazing, but when times are bad, they think it's the economy's fault.

Those companies creative enough to survive bad economies generally have a huge advantage at the start of the recovery—they are usually the first to sense the recovery and the best positioned with resources.

During a good economy there will usually be a lot of competitors trying to enter profitable spaces; in bad economies there is often a higher barrier to entry. For example, we built our trusts and estates practice during good times, when people were planning families. When the economy turns downward, though, people have less to spend on legal planning—which is why we also built a bankruptcy practice, which customers are more likely to need during tough times. Either way, we're trying to help families with all that they need.

How can you insulate your business against this up-and-down cycle and even take advantage of it? Is there an additional product or a new kind of customer that might lead to revenue no matter what the larger economy is doing?

I know I say this a lot, but it is really that important. Keep your personal costs down so you can survive during lean times.

BATTLEFIELD #3: UPSTREAM VERSUS DOWNSTREAM BUSINESS POSITIONING

So you found out where you are on the map (emerging versus mature versus dying market). Then you determined the weather, by thinking about what season you are in (bull or bear market). Now you are going to see how things "flow."

Every business is part of a supply chain. And businesses tend to be in either an upstream or downstream position.

An upstream business captures customers and funnels them downstream to vendors. Upstream businesses (with exceptions) are often commodity businesses, with little to distinguish them, lower-margin products, and expensive customer leads.

> There is no such thing as a bad economy if you have the foresight to position yourself correctly.

My family doctor handles medical checkups for hundreds, maybe thousands, of patients. For special care, the family doctor makes referrals to specialists. When I tore my Achilles tendon, I was referred to an orthopedic surgeon. I had no idea who the orthopedic surgeon was; I just trusted whomever my family doctor sent me to.

The family doctor is *upstream*. He captured me and referred me to the specialist.

The orthopedic surgeon is *downstream*.

This is one reason why hospital systems have bought up nearly all the independent medical practices. By buying up family practices, hospital systems consolidated and controlled the upstream service providers—who now make their referrals to downstream specialists within the same hospital system.

Where is your business on the stream?

Ask yourself, Is your business the first touch of the customer? Do you make referrals—does the customer leave you and transact some further business later on? Then you are upstream.

Or is there another business that experiences the first touch and refers the customer to you? Is business funneled from some other source into your fishing net? If so, then you are downstream.

The answer is important for two reasons. First, it can enable you to properly target your customers. People want to feel connected and special, and understanding where your business falls in the stream will help you refine your pitch. Second, the answer helps you know which tools are the most effective—that is, which techniques are best to target your customers and really get to know them.

Targeting

You would not fish in the part of the stream where the fish cannot be found, right? You want to fish where all the fish hang out.

Similarly, you'll want to understand *where* the target is before you deploy your marketing, branding, and sales resources.

The marketing landscape has changed dramatically over the last seventy years. Gone is the 1950s and 1960s Madison Avenue monopoly over the content we consume. Very few businesses continue to have captive audiences to whom they can force-feed content. Today there is so much content out there, you must be intentional toward your target.

Yet waste is rampant when small businesses throw money at mindless billboards, commercials, and sponsored links on social media.

Most side hustlers should not be using these techniques. Keep it simple. Reach out to those in your network. A good place to start is the army you built in chapter two. Focus on educating the people in this network. If you are lucky enough to get someone in your network to give you an opportunity, then demonstrate that you are offering the best solution out there.

If you succeed, ask them to share their experience and the word will spread. If you fail, then apologize for falling short and ask for advice on ways to improve.

> Connect with your supply chain and customers on an intimate level. Get to know them. Be deliberate in spending time with them or someone else will. Ask them questions like "What problems do you foresee a year from now?" and "How can we solve the problem together?" After they recover from the shock, continue the dialogue.

The Japanese word *uen* is a Buddhist term that means "karmic relationship." You have to get close to the customers to understand their needs and pain points. That is how you discover solutions.

I went out there and created an *uen* with each my referral sources and clients. I wanted to be connected with my clients. I still remember the day when I made the decision to accept fewer clients so that I could better connect with my clients on a deep level.

Turning down clients hit my revenue, but I became relationship rich.

Sure, there is a percentage of the population that cares about low cost, but there is a large percentage that cares more about relationships and experience. I targeted that market.

If you are upstream, you are probably trying to reach a very broad audience, one that can be found in many places. If you are downstream, you are probably trying to reach a very narrow or niche audience, one that will likely be reached in fewer ways and in fewer places.

Whether you are upstream or downstream will determine the tools you use to catch your fish.

Tools

Once you know where to fish, you need to decide what fishing method is best, what kind of line and lure will be effective, and so on. No matter what your customers look like, there are amazing tools you can use to reach them.

Once you've defined your target, the next question is how to convert those specific prospects to customers. If you are fishing, once you've decided where to anchor the boat, you have to decide whether to use a net, a fishing rod, or a spear.

- **Net:** There are so many fish that you can just cast a net. Think iPhone release date.
- **Fishing rod:** You have to put out bait and wait for the prospect to come to you. Think someone shopping for a car.
- **Spear:** You have a hyperfocused prospect that you are hunting. Think wealth managers.

In the old days, upstream marketing tools were things like mass direct mail advertising, the Yellow Pages, or twirling a sign for passing cars. These may have worked decades ago. Today? Not so much.

The upstream marketing tools of today are search engines and social media, generally working in this order: social media pulls the prospect to your website, your website generates a phone call, and the phone call gets you a meeting.

Customer expectations today are really high. You have to execute and provide a great customer experience. Gone are the days of the "good ol' boys club" relationships that were the key link between upstream and downstream businesses. There is too much expectation and competition. You have to execute.

Customer expectation has been shaped by many other areas of life. Click a button, and boom—your dinner shows up. Whatever business you are in, this is the new benchmark you are measured against.

Today upstream businesses are under great pressure to connect customers to people who will provide great product and service *experiences*.
"Just good enough" is no longer good enough. Further, as with hospitals
and family practices, upstream and downstream businesses are increasingly
consolidating, either to balance out profit margins or to control customers.

Technology has empowered upstream businesses as never before;
upstream businesses now control the customer and build our downstream
products and services.

I obsess over the question "Why?"

"Why?" I drive my wife and business partners crazy by constantly
asking this question. Pretty much on a daily basis, I want to know why.

Why do I want to know why?

The goal of a business is to make money. You make money by providing the best-value solution to a customer problem. You need to
constantly ask the customer what their problem is to determine the
best-value solution and make sure you are offering that.

For example, I wanted to know if timing affected customer
demand. I noticed that every December our estate planning revenues
would go up. Estate planning includes the preparation of wills, trusts,
and powers of attorney. These documents are needed to protect your
surviving loved ones if something unexpected happens to you, such as
death or incapacity.

I wanted to know why revenues would go up at this time, so I
asked. I discovered that people were home for the holidays with loved
ones and free time.

In February, our revenues would plummet across the board. I
wanted to know why, so I asked. The answer? Essentially, we are in
Chicago, and it is really cold in February. People are hunkering down at
home or flying south for warm-weather vacations.

You need to know the reasons behind fluctuations so you can
make informed decisions. If you looked at our revenue from February

alone, you would think we need to cut costs to survive, but I am investing big in February. I know that once March comes, the spring market
hits the real estate industry, and we need to be staffed accordingly, to
handle the closing volume.

When you are a new small business, everything depends on you.
You will need to make fast decisions. When you first start your business, so much depends on revenue because you need the cash flow
to survive.

Why am I obsessed with the question "Why?"

The reason is simple: it helps me forecast so I can properly understand my battlefield and the position my business should take. Every
answer to the question "Why?" is a data point on my ever-evolving
analysis of our battlefield.

PLAYING THE BATTLEFIELD

Once you understand all three battlefield factors, you can start to see how
they interact. For example, an upstream market could become a downstream market due to some emerging technology. Or a downstream market could shift to upstream due to a bear market. And so on.

I know this chapter offers a lot to digest, but I think all side hustlers
need to know these conditions to identify new opportunities. Changing
conditions always create new opportunities for hungry side hustlers to
come in and take market share from incumbent players who are not keeping their fingers on the pulse of the customer.

Around now is when things start getting really fun. If you made it
this far, your side hustle must have some legs. But your side hustle is not
the destination. It is just the beginning of your journey.

As with fighting in a martial arts tournament, you need to understand the characteristics of the arena you are competing in. Business is
a contact sport. Your competition is trying to feed their families and the

families of their teammates. Either your family eats or their family eats. Keep that in mind.

Anyone can sail in calm waters, but if you cannot navigate through a storm, your ship won't last. As your journey continues, you may come across new opportunities. If the right opportunity comes along, you may want to flip to or expand into another side hustle.

Just remember: anyone can walk through a calm field on a warm sunny day, but only a well-disciplined army can march through storms while under attack. To build a sustainable business you must be prepared for all battlefield conditions.

PRACTICE TIP

Know Your Universe

The first six chapters of this book focused on you and getting to know your side hustle. This chapter is really about getting to know the environment in which you are operating. You need to know how the specific universe of your business functions.

You would not want to play chess without knowing how the pieces move, right? How can you expect to engage in business without knowing the rules of your game?

Every battlefield is different. In addition, new technology is completely changing the battlefields we engage in. The following is a default approach to analyzing your battlefield:

Step 1: Start with the top competition. Study the top five to ten players in your field. Ask and answer this question: How do they deliver value to the customer, and what makes them different? See what everyone else is doing. Is there something in the process or product that you can improve on that would be important to a certain customer segment?

Step 2: Ask why. Do an in-depth analysis of the top competition. Ask and answer the question, Why do they deliver to the customer the way they do? Normally, when you ask why in this direction several times, you will uncover the rules of this universe. For example: Are there laws and licenses needed? Are there supply chains? Are there labor problems, cost problems, or logistical problems? As you uncover each answer, you need to explore, investigate, and understand each layer of why.

Step 3: Ask: Is this what the customer wants? Put yourself in the customers' shoes. Is there something you can do to improve the customer experience that does not break the rules of the universe? What will set you apart?

Step 4: Relentlessly seek solutions. You have to become a student of the game. Your appetite for information about your field should be bottomless. Read anything you can get your hands on; take classes; listen to podcasts; watch videos; interview experts and thought leaders. The list can go on and on.

There are some who like to start with learning all the rules of the universe and then move on to learning about the top competitors. I think this is backwards. A bishop chess piece is an inanimate object. By itself it does nothing on the chessboard, but for the right player it is a powerful tool.

It is all relative. A chess piece is only as powerful as the person moving it.

The same principle is true in business. An industry is only as powerful as the players running it. Start with the incumbents and work your way back into the universe to find your place.

Now this gets very tricky if you are the first person in a space or if it is a new space. But most side hustlers are playing in established fields.

You must know the waters you plan to fish.

CHAPTER 8 ☯ NEW WEAPONRY

The third step toward stabilizing your business on the Tao of the side hustle is to choose the right weapons.

IN MARTIAL ARTS, A WEAPON IS CONSIDERED TO BE AN extension of your body. If you wield a sword, it's merely an extension of your arm; it extends out past your hand, but it is still subject to the movements of your wrist. A weapon's purpose is to enable you to perform more effectively and more efficiently in combat. The weapon is there to enhance your martial arts ability.

Different weapons can be more or less useful in different combat conditions. For example, to be the one person with a sword in a roomful of sticks and stones is to be king, but to be the person with a sword in a roomful of guns is to be defeated (or worse).

Just as you would not use a hammer to turn a screw, or bring a knife to a gunfight, you must first recognize your setting and then find the appropriate weapon. Choosing and using that right weapon in the right setting may determine your success.

There are various weapons you can acquire to enhance your business ability. When you started this side hustle journey, you might not have had the resources to get newer, better weapons. When you started, you were in survival mode. But when you are stabilizing, you should start looking for new weapons to deploy to improve the way you solve your customers' problems. And often the best new weapons you can provide your army are those you create yourself.

There was once a great Viking king named Bjorn. King Bjorn was the greatest of all Viking kings in battle. He fought off all invaders and kept his lands safe.

He had three sons, whom he was grooming to take over all his lands. His two eldest sons, Erik and Arne, were poised to follow in his footsteps. They were just as big and powerful as their father. They trained their whole lives to lead their people in battle. Prince Erik and Prince Arne always made King Bjorn very proud.

However, King Bjorn's youngest son was born small and weak. King Bjorn hated how weak his youngest looked. He named this son Fluga for "fly." Fluga's mother always tried to love all three of her boys equally, but when she was not around, there was no hiding that Fluga was the smallest—and least loved—of the three brothers.

Unfortunately, the queen fell ill and her life was cut short. On her deathbed the queen made all three brothers take a blood oath that they would protect each other. The brothers agreed.

King Bjorn became miserable after the death of his beloved wife. In addition, the soft touch of the queen was no longer around to keep the enemies at bay through diplomacy. King Bjorn knew only war. Many enemies began to threaten him.

The king called his three sons into his hall. As they knelt in front of him, Bjorn said, "War will soon come to our doors. Prince Erik and Prince Arne, begin to run exercises with your troops." They both stood up and saluted in acknowledgment.

Prince Fluga stood and asked, "What would you have me do, sir?"

King Bjorn said, "My goodness. My love for your mother kept you around. I am sorry, but you are too weak to help here. I am banishing you to the stables. You will groom the horses and prepare them for soldiers."

Princes Erik and Arne, to honor their blood oath to their mother, tried to speak up. But King Bjorn quickly said, "Silence! Your promise to your mother does not overcome my command." They both sat back down.

Princes Erik and Arne prepared their troops for battle, and Fluga was sent to the stables. Fluga arrived at the stables completely deflated. He began to sob uncontrollably. He was greeted by an old man who was blind in one eye. The old man said, "Don't worry, we do not have to pick up the manure until tomorrow. Cry then."

Fluga said, "My father just banished me to the stables. I am the first prince assigned here."

The old man sat down and said, "Well, when I lost my eye I was banished here too. At least we have that in common."

Fluga said, "My name is . . ."

The old man stopped him and said, "I know, Fluga. Your father asked me to train you."

Fluga said, "Train me at what? My father is the cruelest human being I ever met. I hate him."

The old man laughed and said, "Yeah, he is a real son of a gun. But he was nice enough to name you Fluga. Do you know that means 'fly'?"

Fluga said, "Yes, I know. He has terrorized me my whole life. What are you to train me in?"

The old man said, "Swordsmanship and war."

Fluga laughed and said, "You are a crippled old man. What could you teach me?"

The old man stood up and said, "Do you want to train or not?"

Fluga nodded in agreement.

The old man said, "Come first thing in the morning to clean up, and we will start."

The next day Fluga showed up and was given instructions to start cleaning. While he was cleaning, the old man snuck up behind him and said, "Hey, turn around." Fluga turned around, and the old man punched him right in the face, knocking him unconscious.

Every day the old man would sneak up and try to attack Fluga. Fluga made every move looking out for a strike from the old man. As the years went by, the old man taught Fluga how to take care of the horses. Fluga eventually learned to speak to the horses with his hands. In addition, he moved swiftly out of fear of the old man's attacks. Fluga avoided conflict so well that he became impossible to hit.

One day Fluga heard that his brothers had been ambushed and kidnapped. King Bjorn came to see his youngest son. King Bjorn immediately attacked Fluga with a sword. The mighty King Bjorn swung with fierce swings, but he could not land a blow to the swift, elusive Fluga. Fluga made a call and a horse came to his aid. Fluga took the high position and disarmed his father.

Fluga said, "Father, I have been waiting my whole life to strike you down. Why did you give me this cursed name?"

King Bjorn said, "I love you, my son. I saw that you were small. I named you Fluga to make you tough. I knew your spirit needed to exceed your body. And now I have come to see if you are ready."

Fluga threw down the sword and hugged his father. Fluga honored his blood oath and freed his brothers. The brothers saw that Fluga was small in stature but huge in spirit.

King Bjorn passed away, and the three brothers ruled together and there was peace for their lifetimes.

Side hustlers, it does not matter how small you are compared to your opponents. With the right weapons and the speed of a side hustler, you can outmaneuver bigger opponents.

The whole point of innovation is to give your teammates new weapons to compete with. Those weapons may come in the form of new technology or processes. The world moves fast. Your army had better keep up with the competition.

You do not have to win a Nobel Prize to be an innovator. Innovation simply means finding new, better ways of doing things. Anyone can do it.

Here is a realistic approach to innovation for side hustlers.

THE SECRET SAUCE ON INNOVATION

Step 1: Find the bleeding arteries. Identify critical immediate pain points of consumers.

Step 2: Create Band-Aids to stop the bleeding. Create a solution for the consumer—a Band-Aid that offers something a little more than your competitor does but is critical to the customer.

Step 3: Once you identify a problem and propose solutions to that problem, it is time to innovate and iterate to make the solutions better. Look into the future. This step is to try to forecast future pain points and solutions that the consumer does not even realize exist yet. That is practical innovation for your business.

The world moves quickly, and you need to anticipate the next great thing. Nothing is irreplaceable, but if you are constantly innovating and coming up with new solutions, there will always be a seat at the table for you.

Anyone—and I mean anyone—can innovate.

FIND BLEEDING ARTERIES

Start with customer pain points. Everyone has pain that they need relieved. A huge advantage of a side hustle is that you are so close to your customers.

You have to engage with customers to learn how you can make their lives easier. Do not focus on your needs. Focus on your customers' current needs and where those needs will take them. Your business is your customers' business.

I once read a funny case in law school about the will of a person who had left Kodak stock to his heirs. The will said:

> *It is my desire and hope that [the Kodak stock] will be held by my said Executors and by my said trustee to be distributed to the ultimate beneficiaries under this Will, and neither my Executors nor my said trustee shall dispose of such stock for the purpose of diversification of investment.*

This person believed in Kodak so much that he literally told his heirs they had to hold on to Kodak stock. Which may have been good advice while he was alive—but eventually became disastrous.

Kodak was once a brand so strong that we coined phrases after it (for example, "a Kodak moment"). Kodak earned most of its revenue through camera film. In the 1970s it learned about a new technology called the digital camera. It was revolutionary, but Kodak was making all its money from film sales.

Kodak did not give the digital technology the attention it deserved. It was focused on its income statement and not the future of its customers' behavior.

Guess what happened to the sales of film when digital cameras—and then smartphones—came out?

Yup, you guessed it. Kodak ended up in bankruptcy, making the stock worthless. You know something crazy? Even though Kodak was first to the technology by a lot, it did not take advantage of its position.

Kodak became so big that it stopped talking to its customers. Side hustles are almost always talking to their customers. Talk to them and ask them where the pain is.

When your customers talk, you must listen. Once they tell you the pain points, offer a solution.

CREATE BAND-AIDS TO STOP THE BLEEDING

Side hustlers have some huge advantages over bigger companies. Side hustlers are close to the customer and are nimble. Because we are close to the customer, we can identify opportunities (that is, bleeding arteries). After we identify the opportunities, we can quickly work on solutions. We do not have to run them past any committees or bosses; we face no red tape.

Historically, the big, fancy law firms would have very impressive offices in big-city downtown high-rises. Their walls were covered with plaques, Ivy League diplomas, and very expensive artwork. I felt so small next to these lawyers.

However, all that fancy stuff was for their ego, not for the customer.

When I started my side hustle, I was working out of my basement. I would always ask my customers what their biggest pain point was. Almost all of them mentioned that they were time poor, so the Band-Aid that I offered was to meet them at coffee shops near their houses.

I had a great system. I would buy two coffees, handle my client's documents, and move on to the next coffee shop. I can honestly say that there was a day that I drank twelve coffees. The coffee shop should have made me their spokesperson.

Some of my big law firm friends really looked down on this practice and would point out that I was one step removed from making house calls. A dear lawyer friend from a big law firm once said to me, "Sorry, Don, but my clients need to come to me." This is silly. This lawyer was focused solely on their own self-interest, when they should have been thinking of ways to make things more convenient for the customer.

Another lawyer liked to refer to me as "Cheap Labor." I know this sounds crazy, but I always took that as a compliment. I know that I am saving my customers time and money, and I know they value me all the more for it.

TIME TO INNOVATE

As my side hustle began to grow, I started to get more and more referrals. Some of the referrals were customers unhappy with the big law firms. I could not understand why they were coming to me.

I would ask them and they nearly all stated that they hated paying for parking, they hated waiting in traffic, and they hated waiting in the lobby for the lawyer to come get them. They wanted their time back.

I finally got to the point where I was able to afford an office share, and I made sure that I found a location that was not downtown. However, a new technology was introduced that really gave me a competitive advantage over my competition.

Years before Zoom became part of our lives, video teleconferencing with a screen share feature was a life-changing new weapon for my side hustle. My customers loved it and they told all their friends.

Video teleconferencing allowed me to talk with my clients, and they did not even have to leave their home to go to a coffee shop. In fact, the screen share feature allowed me to go through documents with the clients line by line.

I was not only saving them time but giving them a more thorough understanding of what they were signing.

Meanwhile, my competitors kept their fancy offices with $50 parking fees.

Start with the needs of the customer and back into the technology. Be specific to your customer. Technology can play a part in innovation, but technology alone is not innovation. You innovate by inventing a new solution; if technology can serve as a tool in implementing that new solution, great.

I was innovating by going to my customers, but then a new technology (video teleconferencing) came out, which allowed me to innovate even more.

BRINGING IT ALL TOGETHER

The Japanese word *daishinkai* (broken down, it's *dai*, *shin*, and *kai*) means, in the context of Buddhism and martial arts, "the great ocean mind" or "the all-embracing mind."

Like water, we are all connected and blend into each other. We need to have an open mind when we approach solving our customers' problems. You need to look at their whole life and see where they are feeling the pain. I'll give away my secret here: I focus on the values itemized in the first five chapters of this book: skills, army, time, treasure, and energy.

Those five assets are universally critical to all humans, so I try to start there. In those five categories, how is the customer experiencing pain? How can my product or service either ease that pain or be delivered in a way to ease the pain? The more you listen to your customers, the more they will share with you.

Then be on the lookout for new weapons that you and your team can deploy in achieving that goal. Anyone can do this. In fact, I believe side hustlers have a huge advantage here, because of their speed and agility.

———— PRACTICE TIP ————
Your Next Weapon

Throughout the years, many people have asked me why I chose to learn rope dart. It is such a random and rare weapon. It is not very practical in everyday combat, and finding coaches who train in it is almost impossible.

The answer? Audiences at competitions where I used to compete loved it. I started with the customer. Let's find your next weapon.

Step 1: Talk to the customer. I want you to reach out to your top customers and have coffee or lunch with them. Ask them how they are doing and if there are any pain points they have. Then look at the technology out in the market to see if there is anything you can offer to relieve these pain points.

Step 2: See if there is technology that exists that will improve their experience. For me, the technology finally caught up, which allowed me to do almost everything remotely. If the technology does not exist, you can either make it or improve the experience.

It might not even be technology. You do not have to invent the next great app. Maybe it is just improving a process.

Let's say you are a hairstylist. Before the global pandemic, most hairstylists fought through traffic to get to their shops. They would sit around waiting for clients. In addition, they would have to pay rent to the house and carry the overhead for equipment.

When the pandemic hit, my stylist called. Her salon was shut down and she had no idea how she would make money. I asked her if there was a way for her to come to my home and cut my kids' hair in the backyard. If she could do it in a safe manner, I would pay her double.

She created her own process for remote haircuts. Guess what? I was not the only one willing to pay double to save time. Her business exploded in popularity. Except this time, instead of working *for* someone, she operated her own business with low overhead.

Step 3: Try it. My hairstylist had to figure it out through trial and error, but her biggest problem soon became the one we all hope for: she was so in demand that she was overbooked. To improve the experience, she brought on other hairstylists she'd worked with and trusted. None of them paid overhead any longer. Their earnings were pure profit.

CHAPTER 9 ☯ FORTIFY YOUR CASTLE

*The fourth step toward stabilizing your business
on the Tao of the side hustle is to fortify your
castle. Every castle will eventually be attacked.
You must be ready to defend yours.*

NOW THAT YOU'VE BUILT SOMETHING, YOU MUST BE PRE-
pared to protect your creation. It's probably only a matter of time before
another hungry person just like you comes along and considers taking a
piece of your business.

I watched myself get wiped out by do-it-yourself tax return prep companies. I watched myself get outclassed by a younger generation of martial
arts motion capture professionals. I watched myself outpace the old lawyers with new technology.

Any time you build something, there is probably someone right
behind you looking to crush you.

The walls of your castle must be high enough to protect you from
both the incumbents you've been disrupting and the next generation of
side hustlers who will see you as the incumbent.

Your competitors do not care about your needs. Neither does the market, which is cold and efficient. You can be loved one day and hated the next. It is always better to be useful than cool.

So how can you fortify your business and prepare for the inevitable?

There once was a kingdom at the edge of a great mountain range. Legend had it that a little girl who was raised by wolves lived in the mountains. Over the years, many hunters claimed to have seen a fierce, beautiful young woman hunting with the wolf packs on desolate mountainsides. But nobody had ever been able to prove her existence.

One day the king received alarming news: a rival kingdom planned to attack. The king called his son, Tian, who had never been tested. The king had grown old and was no longer strong enough to fight alone. Oddly, the king remembered the legend of the wolf girl and began to think.

The king said to Tian, "Go to the mountain and capture as many wolves as you can. Use them to find the wolf girl, then bring her to me."

Tian traveled to the mountains with a group of men and soon captured several wolves. That night, he was awakened by a loud *thwomp*—the sound of a spear planted next to his head! He opened his eyes to see his men tied up and another spear before his face. A beautiful woman with a menacing face stood over Tian.

"Release my brothers, or I'll have your head," she said.

Tian replied, "I'll release your brothers. I'm not here for them. I'm here for *you*—to bring you back to the king for an audience."

But the woman answered, "I care not for your king. I'd prefer to turn you into a kebab for my family to feast on."

"I beg of you to come with me," Tian replied. "You may defeat me, but if I do not return with you, many others will come and terrorize you."

The woman, whose name was May, had seen hunters before and knew that many hunters with guns would be a problem.

"Then I, alone, will come with you," May said. "Release my brothers and let's get on with it."

As soon as the king saw the woman, he rose from his throne. "Oh, great wolf warrior," the king cried, "you've come just in time. Our kingdom will soon come under attack. Please, you must lead our troops to stop the invaders!"

Tian heard this with great surprise; he had hoped that one day he would lead the kingdom's armies.

May, on the other hand, was unimpressed. "Why should I get involved?" she asked. "Man is a virus. All you do is take. All of you are my enemy. Why should I take sides among you?"

The king replied, "Perhaps. But we are the enemy that you know and thus can manage. We have always respected your borders. The new enemy probably will not."

May considered this. She understood the logic. "Move your people to the top of the mountain and hide them," she said. "When this new enemy attempts to climb the mountain, my family and I will surprise them with an attack from the high ground."

The king did as May instructed. When the invaders came, May and the wolves destroyed them in battle. Badly defeated, the remaining invaders retreated.

During these days, May and Tian fell in love. May approached the king and asked to marry his son.

"I agree to this marriage and give you my blessing," the king said. "I love my son and did my best to protect him and give him everything I never had. However, there is one thing I was never able to give him."

The old king took May's hand. The two felt each other's hands. In the king's hand, May felt the type of callus that comes only from thousands of swings of a sword. In May's hand, the king felt the type of callus that comes only from thousands of thrusts of a spear. They immediately connected.

The king said, "I never gave him the calluses of a hard life—the greatest gift a parent can give a child. A diamond is made only with pressure."

To fortify your castle, you must allow your business to develop the calluses it will need to be durable and resilient to the winds of change. A way that you can achieve durability and resiliency is by becoming irreplaceable.

So far, your side hustle has been all offense. Now it's time to think about defense.

The next step for you and your side hustle is to become *irreplaceable* to your customers and clients—for them to begin to believe that you will always provide the best-quality goods or services—so they stop considering new alternatives.

Athletes watch videos of each other to study strengths and weaknesses, and people in business make similar assessments. My competition simply observed my blueprint and immediately began adopting the innovative new practices my customers liked.

Money will change the perspective of others really fast. My competitors, even the big shots, started to see that certain techniques of mine were working and my customers and revenues were going up.

I had the advantage of being first, but every time I came up with a new idea, my competition was right behind me trying to replicate it. Except that they had a bigger budget to deploy.

When my competitors started seeing that clients hated traveling downtown, they leased satellite offices so there was no need to meet in a coffee shop. When my competitors started seeing the effectiveness of video teleconferencing, they started doing it with fancy lighting in their fancy libraries.

Every time I did something that worked, my competitors were right there to adopt my best techniques and improve on my flaws.

BECOME IRREPLACEABLE

After I realized that my competitors were right on my heels adopting my best practices, I knew I had to keep moving. I turned to educating my customers.

Historically, my competitors charged for content (at hourly rates)—they acted as knowledge gatekeepers and had the leverage to do so. Part of the lawyers' value proposition to the consumer was their knowledge base of the law. Back in the day, if you wanted to know the law, you had to go see your local lawyer. Customers wanted and needed to be educated, and the incumbents charged for this.

However, the internet changed the ways people seek information. Websites began publishing free information. Got a question about the law now? Your first stop is a search engine. The internet knocked down the gate of the lawyers' value proposition of knowledge.

This did not mean that lawyers were going to go out of business. It just meant that the consumer was going to come to the table with a very high level of knowledge.

There is no stopping this evolution. Back during the 2008 crash, I began providing content for free, as a form of marketing. It worked. The fact that I was willing to stand by my positions publicly had a big impact on the consumer. I literally put my name on the line.

Content marketing is not new, but the consumer demand for it is new. Consumers have a huge appetite for knowledge.

Offering free content was incredibly effective (and disruptive) at first. But before too long, my competitors began doing the same thing.

So I had to differentiate myself in another way. I turned my attention internally to processes, in order to improve the customer experience.

I know this idea is not new in the world, but it was very difficult to do in the professional services industry. I was not making the Model T car with replaceable parts here; I was trying to streamline a process while maintaining a personal touch with customers who had a range of different needs.

I was heavily influenced by the medical industry. It really had a streamlined process down to a science. On a basic level, this is how the medical process looks to the customer:

Step 1: You enter the medical office and are greeted by office staff who prepare you for a process.

Step 2: You first interact with a nurse who gathers all initial information. The nurse then feeds this information into a computer for recordkeeping and to update the doctor.

Step 3: Finally, a nurse practitioner or doctor comes in and either deals with the issue or prepares to send you to a specialist. The time they spend with you is very limited relative to the whole process.

You see how the doctor delegates all nonmedical advice work? And then comes in at the end to provide value only the doctor can provide?

This approach allows the doctor to be laser-focused on their true value proposition of patient care. The doctor avoids burning unnecessary mental calories on the administrative stuff. When they are in front of the patient, they are completely focused on diagnosis and solutions.

I wanted the same focus on my true value proposition.

> Your process does not have to be the best in history. You just need to outpace your competitors. Think of ways you can make your process smoother and faster using your competition as a benchmark.

I looked to the medical industry's approach in creating my system. I was the initial touch, making the customer feel comfortable. I then passed the customer to a senior paralegal or associate attorney to guide the customer through the execution of documents. I would be there overseeing the entire process in case I needed to troubleshoot issues. Once the work was done, I would be there for the delivery of the final product. The process saved so much time and improved the quality of work dramatically.

Once I got my system down, I noticed that my competitors were watching closely—both the past incumbents and now a number of new players too. They fairly quickly copied my blueprint and even tried to hire away my employees to implement it. This is harder to actually do than to talk about, but it was both nerve-racking and fun watching them try.

When you get to this point on your side hustle journey, laser-focus on your true value proposition to the customer. Delegate everything else to avoid burning yourself out. Then give the customer the best value by focusing.

All of these experiences led me to a realization: every innovation would probably give me only a temporary advantage.

What I really needed was something permanent.

It was then that I decided to become irreplaceable.

The way to become irreplaceable to your customers and clients is to make it clear that it will be *you* that solves each new problem. The message you want to give your customers is that you will constantly innovate to come up with better ways to solve their problems.

There is a cost to switching companies, brands, or service providers. If your customers or clients are confident that your products will always be at least as good as any competitor's, the cost of switching will seem too high, and unnecessary. Once they believe that your business will be at the leading edge of innovation, providing all that any competitor would be able to provide, not only will they not switch to a competitor, but they'll lose interest in even considering competitors, which frees up their time and money for other activities. It's truly a virtuous cycle.

The way to do this is by constantly developing new value propositions for your customers. The way you do that is by focusing on their needs. And the way you learn their needs is by listening. I would blatantly, bluntly ask my customers what I could do to add more value for them. "What can we do better, more, or differently that would provide you with a better service or product or experience next time? How can we enhance the value of what we're providing?" Then I'd actually listen to the answers, and incorporate their feedback into our processes.

Generally speaking, to become irreplaceable to your customers, you must be focused on solving the problems of today and the problems of tomorrow that they might not even know about.

EXPLORATION

Soon after my small business stabilized, I realized that I needed to seek new paths.

Say what?

Here's what I mean. Humans are naturally explorers. Once you've built up your business, the next phase for you is to begin exploring where the business will go in the future—where customer needs and desires, competitors, technology innovation, economic conditions, and so on will intersect and interact and how your business can evolve accordingly.

The Japanese word *shintei*, in martial arts and Buddhist contexts, means "the ultimate truth." The ultimate truth is that people change and problems change. You can assume that the most urgent problems you are solving for your customers when you first start your side hustle will seem less urgent over time, and eventually might not even be problems any longer. Nothing lasts forever.

To become irreplaceable does not mean you have permanently fixed a problem. Your competition will find ways to improve and replicate. Rather, you must learn to foresee the problem your customer will face before it hits, and constantly work to improve and enhance your solution. In martial arts, the techniques and genetics of opponents change. You must evolve with those changes or you too will risk becoming the next horse and buggy.

My next step on my Tao was identifying those new problems to be solved before my competitors did—really, before my customers were even crystal clear in defining them! I did this in large part by getting back to basics. I started having coffee again with critical partners and thought-ful clients. Not to pitch business but to shut up and listen. Rather than narrowly focus them on the problems we'd already solved for them, I asked these clients about their new pain points, the issues they had started having and couldn't quite figure out and certainly weren't able to solve.

What I got in return was worth its weight in gold. Literally, in real time, I heard the changing needs and problems of my customer base.

I learned that people were sick of lawyers who only knew how to do one thing. They would ask their lawyer a question and the lawyer would always say, "I do not do that." People wanted someone with a broader value proposition. As a CPA I could provide tax advice, but my customers wanted me to learn more. Specifically, they wanted me to learn estate planning (wills and trusts) to help with succession planning and corpo-rate law to help with their small businesses.

With this feedback I began side hustles in wills and trusts and cor-porate law with the *exact same* blueprint, in the exact same chronological order, I laid out in this book in chapters 1–8.

I kept doing it and it kept working.

As my value proposition expanded, I did not want to go too wide. For example, I wanted to stay out of criminal law, but I wanted to go into things connected to real estate closings. Wills and trusts and corpo-rate law were a natural next step. My customers loved that I was able to provide broader advice about their property needs and maneuver quickly between all these services.

Look at your side hustle. See if there are products or services related to your core that you could offer without diluting your current value.

Listening to your customers is not always pleasant. I remember once taking a customer out to dinner after he had left a very bad online review. The reason I was so interested in meeting and talking to this person is that he had very valuable information for me. He did not hold back on how he felt.

In other words, I met someone who despised me just to ask him what we could have done to make him stop hating me. This person gave me great insight on ways for me to improve. Empathy for the consumer made me irreplaceable. I wanted to learn how to make the experience better.

I listened to his pain and apologized for the experience. However, after the customer was done talking, I explained the reason for the pain. His case was a special circumstance, where a random variable, something out of my control, was involved. I did not make an excuse. I simply provided a reason for the bad experience.

Guess what? He took down the bad review. He discovered I was not the reason.

(This will not always work.)

Ultimately, business is about fulfilling people's needs in exchange for their hard-earned money. You're not going to learn what those needs are unless you get out and talk to people. You're not going to find the answers online, on social media, or in a book. You're only going to learn what people need by talking to actual people.

Focusing on exploration significantly helped my business. It allowed me to pay attention in a highly intentional way. It also helped me pay attention to life more. In this process, I learned more about myself and what I wanted. Eventually, we created new lines of business to complement our core competencies. This broadened our value proposition, made the business stronger, and led to more profits.

All from shifting my focus and creating and walking new paths.

> I once met with a powerful Hollywood television executive—a former network head. I asked him for advice. He said, "Keep your antennae up, and wait for your opportunities. Life is like running face-first into a brick wall. At first you get knocked down, but over time you'll learn to either climb over it or break right through it."

PRACTICE TIP

Protect the Carrots

Earlier I told you to look at the incumbents of your industry and find ways to beat them by improving on their processes. If I am telling you to do this, you can be sure that others are getting that advice as well. You have to become irreplaceable by finding new and better ways to solve your customers' problems.

When you started your side hustle, your most important role was to understand your customers' current needs and to sell a product to meet those needs. When you want to grow your business, your most important role is figuring out your customers' future needs, then managing the business toward that.

If you are growing carrots in your garden, you had better immediately put up some deer netting to keep the rabbits out. If you don't, you will work hard to grow those carrots, just to have some rabbits come nibble all of them. The same goes for your business. As you grow, you need to immediately fortify.

Step 1: Grow your business. When you transition your side hustle to a small business, growth is really important. You need those revenues to reinvest into the business and keep the merry-go-round going.

Step 2: Improve the process. Once you have enough capital that you are not worried about making payroll, stop focusing on growth, and focus on quality. You want to make the transition from perceived value to actual value. This keeps your clients around.

Step 3: Find new solutions. Once you perfect your process, assume your competitors are learning your process. Do not be stagnant; keep growing by finding new solutions.

I knew a chef, tired of the long hours of working at a restaurant, who started a side hustle cooking in his kitchen. He started with pre-prepared meals for busy professionals. He focused on profit first with super-low overhead, then eventually expanded to a ghost kitchen. He evolved. He solved the problem of time (chapter three) by easing his customers' need to shop and cook. While cooking for his customers, he discovered that many of them were looking for healthy options to avoid fast food. So he pivoted and made sure his pre-prepared meals were also healthy. He solved the problem of energy (chapter five) by providing something good for the body.

See how he started by solving one problem, but then began solving another problem? He discovered this information by talking to his customers. His side hustle grew and expanded, and he now has five full-time employees.

Keep searching for new solutions to your customers' problems. Keep innovating. Keep evolving. It's the best way to both grow and protect your business.

CHAPTER 10 ☯ COMBAT

The fifth step toward stabilization on the Tao of the side hustle is to develop the ability to engage in combat. Avoid combat whenever possible—but when forced to engage, remember that technique and positioning are greater than strength.

MOST FIGHTS ARE WON OR LOST VIA POSITIONING BEFORE you engage. However, there will inevitably come a time when you'll need to engage in one-on-one combat in your business.

No, I don't mean an actual physical fight. I mean direct engagement that feels like a physical fight—it's just as exhausting and just as expensive.

Let me be clear: I don't recommend this. At all. While getting into a slugfest with a competitor makes for great entertainment on television, it's almost never the best option in business. Think about it: When you're fighting with a competitor head-on, what aren't you doing? Focusing on your customers and your business.

It's also rare to get out of a fight without taking a hit. A fight isn't just about knocking someone else out—it's about not taking damage. Again, this has a cost.

So I try to avoid direct engagement with any competitor if I can possibly help it. When done right, most battles are won or lost before they even begin.

Instead of a fistfight, try to focus on *positioning* and *leverage*.

> In ancient times a rope bridge connected the giant jungle world with the human world. The animals of the giant jungle world were the pets of the gods.
>
> Each year the gods required the human world to sacrifice one thousand lives to their animals. If the human world failed to deliver, giant animals would cross the rope bridge and feast on, well, everyone.
>
> For generations, the kings and queens of the human world retained their power by burdening their people with backbreaking taxes. But a family could erase its debts by volunteering its eldest child to be sacrificed.
>
> Families of laborers with no other way to get out of debt to the kings and queens would often agree. This cruel tradition went on for generations.
>
> The Monkey King—a god, not one of the gods' animal pets— became angered over this manipulation and mistreatment by the kings and queens. He decided to transform himself into the form of a laborer and called himself Hanu.
>
> Hanu presented himself to a king and queen and volunteered himself to be sacrificed. He joined 999 other laborers and children, who were loaded on a ship sailing toward the rope bridge.
>
> When the ship cast off, Hanu spoke to his fellow passengers. "We are off to battle," he announced, "and I shall teach you the art of war so you can fight when we reach the giant jungle."
>
> The laborers and children were confused. "We are but laborers, not soldiers. We cannot fight the giant animals," one cried out.

Hanu replied, "Laborers have hands that are callused from working. You are stronger than most. If you think of yourselves as victims,
then victims you shall be. But if you allow me to teach you, you will one
day return to your families."

The laborers were skeptical, but what did they have to lose? They
agreed, and Hanu spent the two-month journey teaching them the art
of warfare. By the time they arrived, all were prepared to fight.

As the coast of an island came into view, Hanu turned to everyone
and said, "Remember, the brain is the greatest weapon." The whole
ship nodded.

As they docked, they could see another island off in the distance,
connected to the first by a rope bridge. There was no sea below the
bridge, just a bottomless void. This was the edge of the human world,
and a fall from the edge was a fall into infinity.

The king of the animal world was a giant tiger so fierce and enormous that no one dared challenge him. But when Hanu stepped off the
boat, he said to the guards, "I challenge the giant tiger in combat. If I
win, we are to be free."

The guards could not believe someone would be crazy enough to
challenge the giant tiger. They suspected Hanu was a dragon spirit.
They stood still in fear.

So Hanu said, "Go. Relay my message. We shall not cross the
bridge until I have combat with the giant tiger."

Upon hearing this, the giant tiger felt rage—rage that he had been
challenged, rage that the sacrifice would be delayed, rage from hunger.
But he realized he was happy to be on the hunt again after so many
generations of being hand-fed his human food.

The giant tiger entered the rope bridge, and Hanu stood at the
entrance on the human world side. The giant tiger was over two hundred feet tall; Hanu looked like a flea next to him.

The giant tiger laughed as he approached. He said, "I grant your
wish of combat. But I have an offer. If you surrender, I will spare your
life and make you my pet."

Hanu replied, "When I am older and tired, I will concern myself with treaties. For now, I want war! There comes a point when the only solution to clean up a mess is a sword." And with that, he pulled out a small, rusty sword.

The giant tiger laughed again. "That will not work on me," he chuckled. "It cannot even pierce my skin."

But Hanu thrust his rusty sword into the nail of the tiger's paw. The giant tiger roared in anger and leapt at Hanu.

Hanu avoided the sharp claws and began to run. As he ran, his eyes began to glow yellow. The giant tiger, fierce with rage, ran and clawed and lunged. But Hanu ducked, jumped, and outran the beast. The laborers and guards watched in shock.

Hanu ran onto the rope bridge, the giant tiger in close pursuit. Hanu led him all the way to the center of the bridge, then turned and cut the rope. The giant tiger, realizing he'd been tricked, tried to turn around. But the rope bridge snapped. Just as Hanu transformed back into the Monkey King, the giant tiger slipped off the end of the bridge and fell into the infinite void. This is why legend says the tiger spirit is everywhere.

The Monkey King started laughing hysterically, his tail now wrapped around the end of the bridge. The guards threw down their weapons and fled.

To the laborers, the Monkey King said, "Now go back and free the others. You are strong from years of work, and your kings and queens are weak from generations of inheritance. You now have a weapon greater than any sword the kings and queens have. You have your mind."

The laborers returned. They took back the rule of their land, and there was peace.

See how the Monkey King used positioning to win the fight? The Monkey King did not use a fist, and took zero damage in the victory. Position yourself for low damage over the long haul. Winning a fight is pointless if your opponent walks away with a pound of flesh.

When the day comes that you do need to engage directly with a competitor, you'll need to know the best techniques for attack. Here are a few of my favorites.

TYPES OF ATTACKS FOR SIDE HUSTLERS

Combat is a very complicated subject. It will vary based on where you are on your journey. The attack and defense of a side hustle is very different from the attack and defense of a big corporation or even an established small business.

I was fortunate to have the opportunity to witness combat in business firsthand while living and working in Seoul, South Korea. Business competition in South Korea takes on a whole new meaning.

They Are Out for Blood

In South Korea, businesses are often organized as chaebols. *Chaebol* translates to "large family conglomerate." In South Korea, family and blood relationships are serious business. Successful businesspeople make legacy plans so that their children will be successors to the family business.

Accordingly, when chaebols compete in business, they are fighting not only for their next meal but for their family honor and future legacy.

With these high stakes, the businesses strive for significant business and political power. I had the chance to watch from the front lines when I interned at a major law firm in South Korea.

From watching the chaebols compete, I knew that I always needed to prepare for combat. I needed to defend my position against my competitors. I never want to fight; I want to focus on my customers. But if a competitor wants to fight? It would be my honor.

Chaebols would normally attack new market players such as side hustlers by undercutting the prices, acquisitions, or laws. Businesses in America use similar attacks against side hustlers.

Price War!

A very popular form of combat used against a side hustler is a price war, in which a bigger, more established company attacks a side hustle by cutting prices. A big company has cash reserves in its balance sheet, so it does not necessarily need profits to survive. Side hustles almost completely rely on profits for survival.

For example, you might have a lemonade stand where you charge $1.00 for a cup of lemonade. A chaebol would come along and charge $0.50 for that same cup of lemonade. It would charge such a low price not because it could profit from each cup, but because it made business sense to simply outlast you and put you out of business.

Unfortunately, this happens here in America as well.

To defend yourself against a price war is to define your value proposition and your target customer early. You should set your price relative to your very specific "value" and a very specific "customer."

That customer will probably get offers at lower prices than what you are offering. Maybe not today, maybe not tomorrow, but at some time they will get an offer. You need to make sure that your value to that person is enough to keep that person from going somewhere else.

Acquisition

Acquisition is another popular attack on side hustlers and small businesses.

Let's say your side hustle has some new technique, technology, or market share. It might be easier for a bigger player in the space to cut you a check and inherit all your assets or get rid of you.

This is a very difficult attack to overcome for side hustlers and small businesses. If someone comes by and offers you a lot of money to hand over your business, it can seem tempting. We are all in this to make money, and if someone is offering you the money that will allow you to skip the grind, it is something to think about.

In the start-up space, building a company for an exit in the form of a sale or IPO is often the goal of the founders.

Side hustlers are different. Side hustlers may not want to exit.

The way to defend against this is to know your long-term goal. Is this a temporary business or is this your life's goal, which you plan to give to your kids like the chaebols discussed above? If you are a serial side hustler and the side hustle that someone wants to buy is not that important to you, then consider the offer. However, if this is your forever company, then don't.

I am an adviser to several start-ups. One of the questions I ask the founders when they are given an offer is, Is this company your *forever* company? I do not believe, for example, that there would have been enough money in the universe to get Steve Jobs to voluntarily leave Apple. It was his life's mission.

The next question I ask is, How much is the offer?

You need to know your worth. Do not sell yourself short. Know the number it would take for you to give up the asset.

Adopt New Laws

Big companies have the money to invest in lobbyists, who promote their agenda to lawmakers. If you do not have a seat at the table to defend your agenda, you should be worried.

For example, legalized cannabis is an emerging market in America. However, the laws for the cultivation, growth, import, export, sales, and distribution vary tremendously from state to state and from state jurisdictions to federal jurisdictions.

The laws make the barrier to entry so high for side hustlers that it is almost impossible. The costs associated with getting a license are very high, so most of the players have deep pockets.

Legislation is a trickier attack to defend against for side hustlers. My suggestion to side hustlers is either to work toward forming or joining an association of other smaller businesses in the field to share the costs of a lob-byist, or to diversify into spaces where this risk is mitigated dramatically.

CONTROL THE SETTING OF THE FIGHT

If you are forced to fight, go out of your way to control the terms of engagement. I believe most fights are won or lost before the fighting even begins. You control the fight by carefully choosing your opponent, loca-tion, and timing.

In martial arts, your targets are your opponent's chin, temple, and back—and you have to defend yours. The chin and temple are soft points, where you can knock someone out. Your back leaves you vulnerable to being choked unconscious.

When you get to a certain level, everyone knows both offense and defense. Good fighters won't be fooled into fighting on your terms; it's very difficult to knock out these competitors.

It's the same in business. Most veteran businesspeople won't be easily knocked out.

For these competitors, you must be patient and focus on the oppor-tunities that will eventually come. You must wait, sometimes for an ago-nizingly long time, for the right place and right moment to strike. Do not just run in on your opponent's turf, wildly punching. Any competent opponent will be ready with a counterpunch and knock you out.

> Sun Tzu was correct in *The Art of War* when he said, "The greatest victory is that which requires no battle."

First, choose your opponent wisely.

Be honest with yourself. Can you win the fight, and at what cost?

If you cannot win, then retreat and live to fight another day. Look at your opponent's weaknesses. Is there a place to attack where they are weak?

For example, if they are so big that they have forgotten their customers and you could offer those customers a better solution, then consider engagement.

Be careful not to wake or provoke a sleeping giant.

If you steal someone's customers, they will not take it well. They might turn around and attack you. At the side hustle level, your defenses may be too weak to handle a war with a bigger company. Big companies have balance sheets with cash reserves. Side hustlers generally rely on the profit of the company to live. A price war can put a side hustle out of business quickly.

I believe it is a better practice to find opportunities that the bigger, stronger competitors have not yet expanded to. This will give you the chance to grow and become stronger in case you have to fight one day.

Choose the location and timing wisely.

The strengths of side hustlers relative to big companies are speed and agility. Your location and timing are pretty simple. You need to be situated right next to the client and be first with solutions.

When it comes to *location*, as a general rule, position yourself in a setting where your strength is put squarely against your opponent's weakness. For example, in my opinion, Japanese judo, Brazilian jiu-jitsu, and good old-fashioned American wrestling are some of the most practical of martial arts, because they are so focused on positioning your opponent. These systems are great for learning to set up your opponent in a place of weakness.

Side hustlers have the advantage of being hands-on with their customers. Bigger companies with several layers from bottom to top are at greater risk of becoming disconnected from their customers.

I am constantly next to my customers. I have the chance to listen to their needs as those needs evolve.

When it comes to *timing*, you have to be first.

When I hear those new customer needs, I work fast to satisfy them. In the beginning, I was doing trial and error on the spot. Some ideas worked and some did not.

Running a side hustle, you are probably more fluid than your larger opponent. You can adapt more quickly and operate with a much higher profit margin than the larger opponents with big overhead.

> As my business grew, my competitors attempted to engage me by trying to show off, by speaking over me, or by claiming to know more than me. Being smart only matters if you are applying that intelligence to a practical solution to your customers' needs. My competitors spent so much time benchmarking themselves, they forgot about their customers.

CONDITIONING

You have to train yourself and your team for disaster. I drive my team crazy by stress testing our operations, but I do this to prepare everyone for the inevitable chaos that will eventually hit.

In martial arts, you train in the basic moves in order to program them into your muscle memory, just in case you need to use them one day. Everyone is tough until they take a few punches to the face. In panic mode, you default to your instincts, your muscle memory, your basics.

The same goes for business. However, I would argue that combat in business is even more extensive. In business, not only do you have to worry about competition, but you also have to prepare for operation disruptions and market disruptions.

Operational and market disruptions are forms of combat as well, except you have no choice but to engage in them.

You have to train for both of them.

If you are not conditioning your team, you will not be prepared when war comes to your shores.

PRACTICE TIP

Bully Proofing

You should always seek to avoid combat. Engaging in it takes away from your focus on the customer. However, if a bully keeps picking a fight, at some point you will need to stand up for yourself. In the end, the only way to handle a bully is to hit back. Bullies need to know that their actions have consequences. In general, try to avoid combat, but if you are ever forced into direct combat with an opponent, here are some strategies.

1. Focus on Your Opponent's Weaknesses

Never fight someone head-on. Find their weakness. Everyone has a hole in their game. Find that hole and run a train through it.

When you are attacking, make sure you angle yourself so your opponent cannot counter your attack.

In boxing, they call this keeping your head off the center line, and attacking with angles. You move back and forth across center, so your opponent cannot lock on to you. You make yourself hard to hit. And at the same time, you move at angles toward your opponent, allowing your own punches to penetrate. If you throw those punches at weaknesses, they can lead to a knockout.

For example, most fights with other lawyers involve money, usually a settlement. But I am both a lawyer and a CPA. When I'm fighting over a settlement with a lawyer, I speak accounting. When I'm fighting with an accountant, I speak lawyer. I focus the conversation on specific issues that I can speak to and they cannot.

2. Conduct a Swarm Attack

When I lived with the monks at the Shaolin Temple, we studied animal techniques. Some animals are predators, after all!

When I do engage with a competitor, I like to engage in a swarm.

One of my favorite predators to watch is the piranha. Piranhas are fish with teeth. They generally attack only other fish, but really, they aren't picky—they'll eat just about any meat.

As piranhas identify their prey and chase it in a group, one piranha will act as a scout. The scout begins to bite at a weak or vulnerable part of the prey. Once the others see that attacking is safe, they will all begin attacking like the scout; they slowly and methodically weaken the prey, until the prey is too weak and compromised to run or defend itself any longer. And then, at that point of weakness, all the piranhas attack and smother their prey.

One added benefit to developing talent in your business is that you create allies with the ability to attack your opponent as a swarm. As a general rule, I allow my teammates and allies to swarm first. This allows me to study my opponent's technique, letting me decide when to launch my own attack, and distracts my opponent so they are not ready for my attack.

For example, when I'm heading into a negotiation or confrontational discussion with a competitor, I generally bring two allies with me and empower them to speak boldly. That way the person across the table, who is usually alone, has to spar with all three of us.

This technique is difficult for most side hustlers, because often when you start, you are working alone. This is yet another good reason to begin building your army even before you think you can afford to.

3. Wait for the Storm

Sometimes it also helps to do nothing and wait for the right storm to hit.

In martial arts there are two broad systems of attack: fire and water. Fire is one-on-one combat—a very expensive and taxing approach. Every time you get punched, you use up a little of your energy.

Water is a situation in which some force comes in and destroys everything, like the way streaming video wiped out movie rental stores. It was a tidal wave! With water attacks, you cannot stop the momentum; you have to either go with the flow or get out of the way.

Most businesses do not plan for change. Business environments change as consumer behavior changes. When that change happens, you need to make sure that you have the appropriate shelter during the storm and that, when the storm is over, you are one of the first businesses to recover in the post-storm new world.

If you see a competitor that is not prepared for an upcoming storm and wants to engage, it might be better to delay the engagement until the storm hits. At that point, your competitor may be too distracted to focus on you.

PART 3

SCALE

LET'S DO A QUICK RECAP HERE. THE GOAL OF THIS BOOK IS to walk the path from salary to profit. Our Tao is the side hustle and is broken down as follows:

Part 1, Chapters 1–5: You pick a side hustle; you launch it; you grow it.

Part 2, Chapters 6–10: You stabilize your side hustle into a full-fledged small business, allowing you to quit your job and breathe.

Part 3, Chapters 11–15: You grow your business further through *scale*.

We're now in the final act.

You don't have to build the next billion-dollar company, nor should you want to. Maybe you just want to make enough money to pay for your kids' tuition.

The Tao of the side hustle is all about walking a path. When you scale, your path goes from a flat surface to an incline. Just as if you were scaling a mountain.

Mountains are a very important symbol in Asian martial arts culture. I have spent a lot of time in some special mountain ranges.

I was first introduced to Buddhism while training as a monk at the Shaolin Temple, a Buddhist martial arts temple located at the base of the Songshan mountain range in Dengfeng, China. We would run up those mountains every day at 4:30 AM as our warm-up. Running up those mountains in my robe with the monks was one way to forget about my life problems.

As I mentioned in the introduction, it was at the Shaolin Temple where I met some of my kung fu brothers from Wudang Mountain. They were visiting there to cross-train. When I later visited them at Wudang Mountain in Shiyan, China, they shared the concept of Taoism with me. I really appreciated their goal of balance and the path to get there as illustrated through the bagua. I respected that they embodied this path so much that they incorporated a special walk in their martial arts training to reflect and remind themselves of the path.

We have been walking a path in this book, and our path is about to change. When you scale, the path goes up.

One must ask the question, Why are so many famous martial arts schools based in the mountains? One reason is the seclusion mountains offer—I mean, some people just want to be alone. But there are also some practical and symbolic considerations.

Practically, the mountains act as a natural defense against attacking forces. The invader needs to climb to attack, giving the incumbent party the high ground and superior conditions.

Symbolically, those mountain ranges represent hard work and perseverance. Going uphill is hard.

I have scaled my side hustle and climbed mountains. I can say that the analogy is spot-on. Scaling your business is just like climbing a mountain.

Scaling means growing your company. Scaling is relative, and before you scale, you need to decide if you should scale and how much. Do not scale just for the sake of scaling. Some businesses were meant to stay side hustles or small businesses, and there is no shame in that.

Mountain warfare requires the deployment of significant resources and is treacherous. You must consider factors such as the steepness of the climb, the climate, and acclimation, while being mindful of hazards such as cliffs. However, should you make it to the top, you will have a high-ground advantage over your opponents.

Here are some questions to ask before scaling.

THRESHOLD QUESTIONS

1. Should you scale?

Climbing mountains is very difficult, and so is growing a business. You need to know your goal. If you are growing the business to make more money, but the service you offer is so localized that there are not enough customers, then it won't work.

Ask yourself what problem you are solving and whether there is a demand for the solution you are offering.

2. What kind of mountain are you climbing?

Climbing a mountain may be a casual hike or a trek up a steep incline requiring special equipment. It all depends on the mountain. You need to make sure that you have the ability and right equipment to climb.

If you climb too high too fast and you are not properly acclimated or you cannot handle the cold winds, you might have to turn around prior to the summit run.

Ask yourself if you have the equipment necessary to climb that mountain.

3. What will you do at the top?

Before you scale, you need to sit down and think about your end goal—an exit, a family succession, or anything else.

Do some soul-searching here. This step of scaling is extremely difficult, and it might not be worth the effort and pain. Talk to your family and really think this through before you move forward.

The pressures of growing may take a toll on you. (They did on me.) If you've found a sweet spot with a side hustle or small business, there is no shame in plateauing.

Ask yourself what success looks like to you.

FINAL ACT

If you decide to continue this path, I offer you the final act of the Tao of the side hustle, which includes mobilizing, marching orders, formations, deployment, and peace. We will continue to walk this path, but be forewarned—this path presents new challenges.

Let's get moving.

CHAPTER 11 MOBILIZE

*The first step toward scaling up on the Tao of the
side hustle is to mobilize. You need to get your
team together and moving in the same direction.*

YOU NEED TO HAVE A SYSTEM IN PLACE SO YOU CAN ASSEM-
ble your troops for duty. A good starting point for creating such a system
is to define your goal and develop a strategy that guides your teammates
to that goal. Once the strategy is set, and maybe even illustrated in the
form of an organizational chart, you can offer your team a purpose and
culture to get them moving in the same direction.

I was very happy in my side hustle. I was making enough so that *I* was
super comfortable. Notice I said only "I."

When my kids were born, my life changed. Doing kung fu was no
longer my top priority. Filming more martial arts motion capture was the
last thing on my mind. I was dealing with dirty diapers and crying babies.

My life became raising my kids. Raising kids is really hard. It is incredibly time-consuming and expensive. I had no idea how expensive it was. The cost of raising a family today is crazy.

When I started my side hustle, the original focus was just survival. To get my next meal, I needed new business in the door—and once it got in the door, the focus was on executing (that is, doing the work).

Then, as the business grew, I needed to hire people to take on some of the work. We grew slowly, one new employee at a time, and became a stable business.

At that point, I knew I had a decision to make. To make more in profits, I could either grow the company more or make it leaner and more efficient. I decided to grow.

I needed to get organized.

Each year I had been hiring people, training them, and delegating responsibility to them. But I realized that to grow even more, I needed to create a *system* for the entire team to work within, so that we were always all moving in the same direction and toward the same goal.

There once was a young prince who was in line to become emperor of his kingdom. He was taught about combat and life by his martial arts *sifu*.

On his sixteenth birthday, the young prince and his *sifu* went for a walk. "*Sifu*, I want to become a just emperor and lead my people to peace and prosperity," the young prince said. The *sifu* smiled, as he knew he had helped build a young man with integrity and character.

Their walk took them along the river, where they saw foreign swamp people fishing along a bank.

The prince scoffed at the swamp people. "I hate seeing these people come onto our lands to fish," he said. "When I am emperor, I will build a wall to keep them out."

The *sifu* dropped his head in disappointment. "Do you know why the Roman Empire fell?" he asked the prince.

The prince replied, "I am not sure. Weren't there invaders? Neighboring nations?"

The *sifu* said, "Yes, but *why*? The Roman Empire was once a powerful empire with a strong army. For centuries, *the Romans* were the invaders. Why did they fall?"

The young prince could only shrug. He had no answer.

"Some believe the Roman Empire grew weak because its leaders did not earn their positions. They were simply the children of powerful prior generations with no real-life experience and no right to rule," the *sifu* said.

The prince replied, "I am willing to go out and earn my place, *sifu*."

"Are you?" the *sifu* asked. "Then I will bring you to the entrance of the bamboo forest with nothing but the clothes on your back. If you make it out the other side, I will teach you how to earn your place."

The prince agreed to this challenge—after all, he had been trained by the best and brightest and had studied survival skills with the best teachers the country had to offer, so the challenge seemed simple enough. The *sifu* brought him to the edge of the bamboo forest.

Soon after the prince entered the forest, the trees became thicker, the vegetation became wilder, and the path became harder and harder to see. Before long, the prince was lost; he could not find the path or his bearings. Still, he walked on.

Suddenly, he felt himself sinking. Without even seeing it, he had walked into quicksand. He struggled, but the sand pulled him lower. He screamed for help, but nobody was near.

He looked up and saw a tree branch, just out of reach. He had an idea: What if he took off his shirt and tried to swing it up to the branch? He did it, and it worked. He was able to pull himself to safety, though his shirt was lost in the quicksand pit.

Night approached. The prince was cold, lost, hungry—and now covered in sand and shirtless. He decided to keep walking to try to stay warm.

On he walked, through that night and for several more days and nights. Eventually, he simply collapsed, starving and exhausted.

Just as his mind was fading to black, the prince heard footsteps. As he blinked open his eyes, the prince saw bare feet before him . . . feet belonging to the swamp people. These people brought the prince to their fire and gave him food and water.

As the prince regained his strength, the swamp people showed him how they used nets to catch fish and woven reeds to catch water, and their other ways of life. Eventually, the swamp people guided the prince out of the forest.

The *sifu* was waiting there. "I see you have met some friends," the *sifu* said. "And what have you learned from them?"

The young prince replied, "I lost everything. I almost starved and froze to death. But these people found me and picked me up. I owe them my life. My first act as emperor will be to build a bridge to the swamp people. Not a wall."

The *sifu* replied, "My son, you are now ready to lead us."

The intent of a system is to get everyone moving in the same direction to achieve a goal. You should design the system in such a way that bridges are created between people so they can all work together.

Note that I use the word *system* intentionally. A process is different—and I'll talk about processes in the next chapter.

When you started your side hustle, you were everything. You were marketing, production, and distribution. Since you were so hands-on, you had your finger on the pulse of everything.

However, if you scale, you need to hire and delegate. To delegate, you have to set expectations for you and your teammates by outlining duties so you can assign tasks.

Before we can talk about a system, let's take a step back and think big picture. Why are we doing this? What is the goal?

THE GOAL

The goal of a side hustle business is to profit. Without profit, the business cannot continue. A side hustle business is not a big company with investors and a balance sheet that can weather years of no profit. A side hustle must profit, or die.

However, this does not mean that profit is the only goal. You should absolutely balance making a profit with social responsibility. You can make money and be kind to the universe at the same time.

In the beginning of the book, I said that there are only so many sword-striking techniques. However, the way you apply those techniques is your interpretation. Your martial art.

It is the exact same in business. The goal is profit, but the way you get there is your art.

Once you've identified the goal, get everyone organized and aligned so they can all move in the same direction.

SYSTEM

The Chinese characters 慧剑 (*huì jiàn*), in a Buddhist context, loosely translate to "the sword of wisdom that cuts through illusions."

Let's try to cut through the illusions. The goal of a business is to make a profit. You make a profit by offering a product or service that offers value to your customer. A system is a way to mobilize your team to deliver that value to scale. Your system should be built around a strategy that delivers that value. The strategy is the plan to deliver that value.

Most side hustlers do not have the resources to develop proprietary technology. Instead, most side hustlers should focus on something that makes them special to their customers, such as relationships or differentiation.

You need to build your system around that relationship or differentiation. The thing that makes you special is the value you need to make sure you deliver.

The people in your organization should all have a role that supports, promotes, or delivers that value to the targeted customer.

For example, when I started my side hustle, my differentiator was going to the client instead of the client coming to me. My strategy was targeting customers willing to sacrifice the bigger, more prestigious law firms for cost savings and the chance to avoid the time and hassle of a commute.

My strategy meant I was traveling a lot. No need for brick-and-mortar offices for me. Since I was traveling to the customer, I was a virtual business that could work remotely from anywhere. I set the roles of my teammates up to support this virtual service by allowing them to work remotely as well.

Once you know your strategy, you can build your system around it. In my case, my system was my laptop, software, and people.

People are the most important part of a system. One way to illustrate the system of people is through an organizational chart. An organizational chart itemizes individuals' roles and duties. I will discuss how to create an organizational chart in the next chapter.

Once your system is in place, get your troops aligned and moving in the same direction with a common purpose and culture.

1. Purpose

Now that everyone knows their roles and their duties, you must show each person their purpose on both micro and macro levels. Show them the reason they exist.

Start on a micro level. Your employees need to know the reason they exist in your universe. They need to understand the intent behind the position you created, for guidance when they are executing tasks. After they understand their role and duties, show them how their role and duties affect others on your assembly line. For example, if you are making sandwiches and the lettuce person puts on way too much lettuce, then that affects all the other people making the sandwiches.

Move on to a macro level. Show your employees how their role will eventually influence the customer experience. Continuing the example of the lettuce, if there is so much lettuce that none of the other toppings make it into the sandwich, the customer will not be happy.

Make sure you're clear about purpose—your company's purpose, and the purposes of individual employees.

> **Ultimately, the system needs to make sure that the roles and duties of your teammates maintain and enhance the value to the customer.**

2. Culture

After everyone knows their purpose, create a culture within the business.

To grow your business, you need to focus your energy in a specific direction to generate momentum. In other words, you need to get everyone moving in the same direction. To get everyone moving in the same direction, you need to create a corporate culture.

Tao means a path to walk. At this point, you must make a Tao for your teammates. You must show them a path to walk.

A culture is more than some statements on the wall. It a mindset. A way of thinking. A *Tao*, a shared belief system expressed in action.

Here are ways I built our corporate culture.

Mission Statement and Vision Statement

To get both sponsorship of (from leaders at the top of the organization) and subscription to (from the rank and file at the bottom) mission and vision statements, everyone at every level needs to see the same clear path forward. Illustrating that path is critical. When people see a map and know where they are going, they get energized. When they are lost, they are hopeless, scared, and unproductive.

As you climb your mountain, you will need to know your point A and point B. Your mission statement is who you are—your point A. Point B is your vision statement: where you want to be in the future. Point A and point B will change over time. Your experiences will change who you are, and your environment will change where you are going.

Core Values and Practices

Your core values are guiding principles—the underlying character traits you fall back on.

For example, my company's core value is trust. Most businesses come down to trust. People need to trust you to do business with you, and they need to trust you to solve their problem.

Trust even extends to your team. For a team to function, its members must trust each other. If that trust is consistently compromised, then the individuals will lose confidence in the team.

You demonstrate trust via accountability. If something goes wrong, you own up to it. At my company, we do not tolerate "throwing each other under the bus" when things go wrong; this compromises confidence in the team. The way we promote accountability is by creating a nurturing environment focused on learning and development.

Consider what fundamental character traits you want to be known by. We default to our basics in a dogfight, and your team will need some guidance on basics they can default to when they are getting beaten up.

Environment

Just as you do not want your kids playing in a sandbox with scorpions, you do not want to work in a hostile or toxic environment.

I have a strict "no a**hole" policy that I enforce with an iron fist. I do not care how much money you have—I do not want you messing up the chemistry of my team or my supply chain. There is plenty of talent and money out there for me to get. I simply will not put up with toxic people.

The Chinese characters 圓海 (*yuán hǎi*), in a Buddhist context, loosely translate to "the all-embracing ocean."

We are all in the ocean together. If there is an oil spill, it affects everyone around you. If someone is toxic, get them out fast!

We once had a referral partner who was something of a big shot; this person sent a lot of business our way. But—despite our requests to stop—this person consistently used derogatory slurs when things did not go his way. This made all the employees feel uncomfortable.

At the time, the idea of severing ties with this person was a really scary proposition with very real revenue implications—this person referred that much business to us.

But I publicly fired this person from our supply chain. Losing his business hurt our bottom line, but it helped our team's chemistry. My whole team witnessed me cutting off someone who was toxic. Over time we replaced these revenues with business from partners more in line with our beliefs and behaviors. To this day I guard my sandbox viciously.

Mistakes will happen. When they happen at my company, we address them. Teammates hold themselves accountable, learn from their mistakes, and then teach others not to make them. We incentivize that behavior. If teammates do not hold themselves accountable or do not learn from their mistakes, we have swift (and sometimes harsh) consequences.

This approach to our environment enhances comradery. Knowing of the incentives and room for growth, teammates have become collaborative and kind to each other. Sometimes they fight over responsibility for problems. The old saying "I am selfish when it comes to claiming responsibility for a mistake and sharing when it comes to praise" has become a real thing on our team.

Find those qualities and characteristics that are most important to you. Rather than trust and accountability, perhaps you value joy. Or creativity. Or integrity. Or kindness. The point is, make sure your entire team knows which qualities you most value, and insist they do the same. Guard those qualities as if your business depends on it, because it does.

This exercise is critical to scaling, because it is the closest thing you will ever get to a true map. When you are climbing a mountain you've never climbed before without a guide, it is really easy to get lost and scared. You will need to know who you are and where you are going so you do not get lost or distracted.

My company is built around trust and respect, as we are focused on customers interested in these same principles. Every action internally and externally should be aligned with this culture. What anchor principles does your company have?

In the next chapter we will discuss marching orders, but here are practical tips for how to formulate a strategy for side hustlers.

PRACTICE TIP
Strategy

SWOT analysis is an important first step to help formulate strategies. SWOT stands for strengths, weaknesses, opportunities, and threats. I believe this is a great exercise for side hustlers when they are starting out. If you have not done this yet, you should do it as an exercise. Take a sheet of paper, draw a grid with four boxes, and list out all the strengths, weaknesses, opportunities, and threats that apply to you and your business.

As you grow, the SWOT analysis may be too linear for practical use. If you are scaling from side hustle to small business, a differentiation strategy may be more practical. Here is a step-by-step way for you to differentiate yourself to your customer:

Differentiation Strategy

1. Ask your customers what is important to them.
2. Ask your customers if the needs they identified are being met by your competitors in the marketplace.
3. If your customer is unhappy, ask what you can do differently to be better.
4. Offer a solution that is different from what is out there. This is where you develop your style.
5. This solution might become your specialty if you:
   a. deliver that solution and your customer likes your solution more than the alternative, and
   b. you find it worth providing that solution and your customer believes it is worth paying for that solution.

You become special to your customer by offering something different that the customer values.

CHAPTER 12 ☯ MARCHING ORDERS

*The second step toward scaling up on
the Tao of the side hustle is to make sure
your team has clear marching orders.*

ONCE YOUR TEAM MEMBERS ARE MOBILIZED, THEY NEED TO know where to march and how to move in that direction together in a coordinated way.

In the previous chapter, we brought your team members together by mobilizing them in a system. In this chapter, we will give them marching orders with processes and controls.

In ancient times, the gods created a paradise where humans and spirits shared the same space. Humans were children of the gods, so they were loved. But some of the children misbehaved.

As punishment, the gods split the universe into two realms, the human world and the spirit world. The spirit world was high above the clouds, and only the worthiest could pass there from the human world.

A legend grew that one could reach the spirit world only during sleep. Elders claimed that pillows could transport humans there—that was why pillows were white, to send you to the clouds—and that it was only during sleep that clues about reaching the spirit world were revealed. If humans died without yet being considered worthy, they would be reincarnated. Some souls were trapped in the human world for hundreds of lifetimes without figuring it out.

A girl named Victoria was born. While pregnant with her, her mother dreamed of climbing a mountain and reaching the clouds; hence, the name she gave her daughter, Victoria for victory.

The gods favored Victoria. They sent hints to her while she slept. But Yama, the lord of the underworld, hated this. He sent his demons to follow Victoria.

Every time the floor squeaked in the dark, she knew the demons were present. But she tried her best to ignore them.

Yama decided to influence Victoria's friends instead. And they in turn began to influence her. Her friends cherished and honored wealth and possessions over kindness and integrity . . . and eventually Victoria did too.

One day Victoria's friends decide to throw their garbage in the river, simply because they could. Victoria stood and watched, and she and her friends laughed at their trash floating away.

That night the river spirit visited Victoria and said, "I have spoken to the gods about what you have done. How do you expect to pass into the spirit world after disrespecting me?"

Victoria said, "Wait, no—it wasn't me; it was my friends."

The river spirit said, "I care not. You stood by, said nothing, did nothing. You watched as they did wrong. You are equally guilty."

Victoria replied, "I have no control over others."

The river spirit sighed. "Only the worthy may pass into the spirit world. If you are not brave enough to point out injustice when inconvenient to you, you will return to the human world in the next lifetime as something . . . less attractive."

Victoria's friends appeared. The river spirit continued, "Since you like garbage so much . . ." Victoria's friends began to transform into rats, screaming and clawing at each other. Victoria started to transform as well. She began to scream . . .

And then she woke up. She never saw those friends again and was much more careful about who she surrounded herself with. She started cleaning the planet, one piece of trash at a time. Victoria was *worthy*.

You need to treat your teammates like family. You would not dump a bunch of garbage on your family, would you? You need to build your system and processes so there is balance and no one gets abused. Too often, leaders do not pay attention to their people and their workflows. Staff gets overworked and abused, which leads to bottlenecks and inefficiencies. Do not put your assembly line on autopilot. You have to pay attention to your team. You have to know your processes intimately to protect your people. Your people are your most valuable asset.

The Japanese word *mushin* translates to "no mind"—roughly, "to act without thinking." This word had a big influence on me when I was creating processes.

To achieve *mushin*, you must create a sequence of moves that your team can commit to muscle memory. If the *mushin* of your team reaches a certain level, your employees will not only execute tasks—they will also start foreseeing problems.

PROCESSES

If someone gives you an opportunity, you need to deliver. I am really passionate about this topic and can go on and on about it, because of how badly I've gotten it wrong. Because I've experienced the devastating impact of not paying attention, I've made it a huge part of my life's work to really understand how to do so most effectively.

A process is a sequence of actions or materials assembled in the chronological order needed to create a desired output. I like to illustrate processes in flowcharts. The flowchart allows us to visualize the way our teammates need to work together.

Work backwards. I like to break down the events that lead to the end product or service into manageable parts for teammates. Each part is a "work center" where the work is done. Doing this allows my teammates to become experts in their respective work centers.

> Processes are sequences of events, which can be replicated, with a predictable outcome. If the outcome isn't predictable, then it's much harder to delegate that work.

At my company, we break down each step exactly the same way I teach martial arts: one move at a time. You need to break down your processes for each operation into tiny sequences at this level of detail. The tinier the steps, the better your employees will be prepared for the inevitable variations.

The goal of a process is to manage "flow"—that is, the completion of an activity at a work center to be sent to the next work center in a sequence.

Why is flow so important at the side hustle level? We already established that cash flows are critical to small businesses. If your assembly line stops flowing, then the cash flow stops. Since cash is like oxygen flowing to your lungs, you need to make sure there is nothing there restricting the flow.

Your job is to constantly watch and improve this assembly line to improve flow. You need to keep things moving at the right pace. Too fast and you create bottlenecks, and too slow and you may not hit targets. You need to time the flow just right. And even after you design the workflow, you have to constantly monitor and improve on it.

Like most side hustlers, I thought my goal was revenue. I was taking in anything that made money. There was no vetting process in place. In the short term, my business appeared to be great.

Revenues were way up, and the work was flowing through my assembly line. It was on autopilot. I was winning, right? I went out and got even more business.

This was a huge mistake.

> Do not accept every customer for the sake of accepting a customer. You want to accept the right customer. If you are letting every customer in, but they are giving your teammates a hard time, then that may not be the best thing. Your revenues might be up, but your teammates will be miserable.

When you are running a race as a team, you must all cross the finish line at the same time.

Certain clients started becoming a problem. The problematic clients were creating too much of a variation in our service; these variations started causing bottlenecks. The bottlenecks began to aggregate, causing all kinds of turbulence and delays. I was not managing my work in progress (WIP). A WIP is an incomplete product or service on your assembly line.

For example, let's say you are selling lemonade at a lemonade stand, and you break up the process into three steps. Step one is setting up the supplies and equipment: water, sugar, lemon juice, a pitcher, and a stirrer. Step two is pouring the water, sugar, and lemon juice into a pitcher. Step three is stirring the ingredients to making the lemonade.

Step two of pouring and step three of stirring are two separate work centers. After step two, the ingredients are there, but not stirred. Therefore, they are incomplete inventory. That is a WIP.

Historically, businesses such as manufacturing companies could manage bottlenecks by limiting physical space at work centers. If there was too much stuff piled up, it was a signal for everyone to slow down.

However, this is harder to do in the virtual world, because there is no physical space to generate a signal for production to stop if a major bottleneck occurs. Without that signal, one functional teammate could keep piling on more work onto another one without even knowing it was too much.

Virtual businesses are different. Since there is no physical space, there are less obvious signals to tell the different work centers to slow down. If there was a problem in my company, the WIP began to bottleneck. (Think a hundred-car pileup on a two-lane highway.) My staff had to muscle through this, and they were overworked and miserable. The delayed customers were unhappy.

It was a mess.

I had a life-changing moment when a dear friend and teammate whom I loved finally came to me in confidence, explaining to me the pain the system was causing everyone. My whole team was ready to just walk out on me. If they left, I would go out of business, because there would be no way I could do the work without them.

When I saw how real this pain was, I took massive immediate action.

I fired all parties—including leaders, clients, and referral sources—who were causing problems to my team by dumping garbage work on my assembly line. This action decreased volume, easing the bottlenecks, but also decreased revenue. I sat my team down and told them that I was turning all my attention to improving flow by balancing output with their mental well-being.

I was honest with them about the decrease in revenues, but I explained the reason I was doing it. Despite all the pain we went through, no one left me.

To fix my bottlenecks, I needed to find the source of the pain. A chain is only as strong as the weakest link. A chair can only support as much weight as the weakest leg can hold.

I gave my assembly line an honest assessment and found my weakest points. Those weak points are the maximum capacity that your team can handle. I had superperformers who were applying too much pressure to the weakest links in the chain. This caused breakdowns.

How did I fix the problem? I focused the superperformers on the parts that needed improvement. In the short term, this forced the parties to be more in sync.

Over the long term, we learned to support the weakest links when we could see they needed help.

In the beginning of this book, I advised you not to try to turn your weaknesses into your strengths. That is only true at the side hustle level. When you grow to a level where you are scaling, you can turn your weaknesses into strengths by assembling and developing your team.

In an assembly line, your weakest links are your top capacity. Over time, you can raise this capacity by strengthening those weak links with better talent or better support.

We created signals to help each other interact when a bottleneck was occurring, so the other parties could slow down production. You need to think about this in your business, especially if it is virtual. Make sure that each team member is in tune with the other team members on workloads.

My goal transitioned from revenues to profitability balanced with quality of life for my staff. You know what happened? No one left, and the team started performing better.

It is bad business to run your team into the ground just to maximize profitability. That is short-term thinking. Always talk to your team. Ask them how they are doing and how you can improve. You will get valuable insights.

Listen to your people. Businesses with systems and processes are like an interconnected organic chain. Bottlenecks are a symptom of a weak link. Your team can give you the information to diagnose and cure the weak link. The weak link may be personnel, the sequence, or an improperly defined role.

Do not work at capacity. Leave some reserve for your team for the inevitable variable. When the variables hit, this will cause a bottleneck. If you do not have a reserve set aside, then your team will only make it through by overworking. Burning out your team to make an extra buck is bad business because you are interfering with long-term flow of output.

If your staff is overworked and miserable, there will be turnover and health concerns. Turnover and sickness destroy productivity.

Your process should keep the flow of output constant and consistent, so you can keep cash flow coming in. If your system or process crashes, then that stops the flow of output, which stops the flow of cash, which suffocates you.

QUALITY CONTROL

Someone needs to check the work. Once your process is created and you start executing it, you need a quality control person to make sure the work being produced is up to a certain standard.

I love the airplane maintenance check before a plane takes off as a gold-star benchmark for quality control checklists. Have you ever been sitting in a delayed airplane and heard the pilot say, "We will take off in a few minutes; our maintenance crew is just doing a preflight checklist"?

No one complains about the delay. If something is wrong, we want to know about it when we are on the ground rather than thirty thousand feet in the air.

Airplane checklists vary dramatically based on company policy for the type of plane and cargo, but generally an airplane checklist breaks down the flight into the actions of the overall process.

The airlines break down the action of the flight (that is, the process) into smaller actions such as pre-start, taxi, pre-takeoff, post-takeoff, approach, landing, taxi, parking, and shutdown.

Then each action has its own checklist. For example, pre-start is checking fuel, lights, engine, electrical, and so on. They have it down to a science.

In the case of your business, break down the process into actions. These actions should offer a deliberate break in the workflow that allows you to check the quality using a checklist.

The items on the checklist should reflect the value you are giving to your customer. For example, in the case of the pre-start airplane checklist, it is important for the pilot to check the fuel levels. Safely landing at a destination is part of the value of an airline. Checking the fuel before taking off supports that value.

Break down your output into actions, and the checklist should support the value you offer.

Over time the repetition should give the parties an opportunity to improve and forecast new values that may become part of that checklist later.

Start at a high, macro level, identifying critical points. Then break down your process at the micro, atomic level, step-by-step, for teammates to follow.

Creating an assembly line requires you to think deeply about your own personal process and approach. You have to extract those individual steps from muscle memory and break them down into the smallest possible component parts.

You need to design checks and balances to catch errors. The steps you design have to be broken down into understandable actions, with specific instructions, to ensure there is uniformity in the product or services you are delivering.

After I would teach a martial arts technique, I would monitor the student to ensure that they were executing it properly. Once I saw that they had it, I would let them practice on their own to get their repetitions in, but I would always eventually come back around to make sure that they were doing the technique within certain parameters.

I struggled with controlling variations and errors in my own assembly lines, partly because in a service business there can be a wide range of problems, with unique aspects that require qualified expertise to resolve.

For example, a lender is involved in the purchase and sale of assets such as businesses or land. The lender is the money, and without the money there is no party. Well, that means I am in the supply chain with finance, and if the lender is delayed, fails to deliver, or does not communicate, then this affects all parties in the transaction.

I could perform at my highest level, but if the money does not show up, I cannot complete my output. The variations caused by delays of the other vendors in the supply chain are my main reasons for bottlenecks. (These are not always the lenders' fault. The lenders are interfacing with multiple parties themselves.)

However, seeing this bottleneck forced me to turn my process into one that was proactive instead of reactive—I learned to get ahead of the issue rather than waiting for the issue to come to me.

I would set internal deadlines for lenders to give me a status. If they failed to respond, I would tell everyone in the supply chain that financing might be delayed. I was not trying to be a tattletale, but trying to give all parties in the supply chain advance notice in an effort to avoid a bottleneck.

I also created intentional friction at certain critical points, ensuring extra attention was given to the matter and the client at those points.

Wait, what?

Why create intentional friction?

Because sometimes activities become so seamless that we switch our brains onto autopilot and don't pay attention. Inserting intentional friction snaps the customer back to conscious attention.

For example, we don't allow something as critical as money-wiring instructions to be transmitted via email (even encrypted email). We make obnoxious signs and warnings to our clients in our emails and retainer agreements. We cause all kinds of intentional friction when it comes to wires, because we want our people to pay attention. We warn them to verify the wire instructions by telephone, independently. To me, it's obvious that the consequences of miswiring someone's funds far outweigh the inconvenience of performing that extra check.

Today's customers do not have much tolerance for mistakes. They work hard for their money, and they want to make sure they are getting the right value for it. Create your own inventory to capture errors. Document, document, document with checklists, checklists, checklists.

EMPLOYEES: NONE OF THIS WORKS WITHOUT GREAT EMPLOYEES

All your processes and quality controls will be meaningless without employees who can apply them successfully—with empathy and judgment—to your customers' needs.

Your employees are the fuel for your machine.

When I was in elementary school, my teachers used to try to stop me from inhaling potato chips. "Stop eating junk food!" they'd say. "You are what you eat!"

As I got older, I realized how right they were. After a stressful day at work, I would reward myself with some alcohol and pizza. The alcohol made working out almost impossible—both that day, because I was drunk, and the next day too, because I would be hungover. The things I was putting into my body? Toxic.

I needed to change my lifestyle. Food was the fuel for my body, and I needed to make sure the fuel I was using was good for long-term performance.

In business, your employees are your fuel. You have to manage the fuel that goes into your machine, because that fuel affects performance.

Hiring

In hiring, I live and die by these words: "the best person is not always the right person." When hiring, I focus on the "right" person for the job. I rarely look at technical skills as the lead factor. Rather, I focus on character.

> Technology, processes, and training level the playing field from person to person when it comes to technical skills. But nothing can overcome certain character traits.

I ask myself, Is this person nice? Are they kind? Or are they a condescending jerk? If the answer to the latter is yes, I immediately turn away, no matter how skilled they are.

I use a three-step hiring process. First, I match the candidate with the position. Does this person have the basic skill set to do the job or to learn how to do the job?

Second, I look at the person's desire to do the job. If they are hungry enough, they will stop at nothing to be great at it. They will be resourceful enough to figure out how to be the best.

Third, I ask myself if the person will get along with my team. One bad apple can spoil the entire pie—it can cause a chain reaction in your system.

Martial arts teaches us that technique is greater than strength and hunger is greater than talent. If that person is not hungry, their talent will eventually diminish.

Choose your people wisely. They not only *reflect* your company but *are* your company.

Retention

Keeping your talent is as important as hiring. You have to illustrate a clear path to success for your employees. In many martial arts styles, there is a color-coded belt system to illustrate a path to mastery (for example, white belt to black belt), and you should create a similar system in your business. People need to feel like they are working toward something. You have to create and present a shared concept that all your employees can buy into—a shared *purpose* that aligns each person's sense of self-purpose with the company's purpose. The problem is, everyone has their own definition of success. So you have to make sure everyone understands yours.

There are five approaches I use to align the purpose of the employee with that of the company.

1. I try to find ways to make my employees feel *vested* in our success—to literally feel a sense of ownership over both day-to-day activities and our long-term success. I want them to feel the same about our work as they would if we were growing fruit and vegetables in a garden—responsible for small details and satisfied with the results of our work.

2. I give *public recognition* to show people how proud I am of them, and this helps people take even more pride in their work. Take the time to make your employees feel good about things they have done. Make them feel special. The world can be a pretty terrible place, so create an oasis for your team to live in while at work. Be kind, even when mistakes happen.

3. I focus on *growth*. The earth is constantly in motion, our bodies are in motion, and our spirits are energy that fuels movement. Humans, like all living things, need to move, change, and evolve. There has to be constant learning and growth.

4. I attend to *happiness*. This tends to be the most abstract and customized—and it takes a lot of legwork. It requires you to get to know each of your people and what makes them happy. Then you see if there are ways to help them achieve personal happiness.

5. I focus on *money*. People need to eat. You need to pay them. I simply do not believe in small companies where the mission appears to be to maximize profits for the owners. I believe you should maximize profits for high-performing employees.

> When the economy goes bad, people get fired, laid off, or furloughed. If that's the result of poor performance, that's one thing, but if these dramatic actions are the result of reduced profits for ownership, that's quite another. You should never eat into the profits of high performers. Invest in your team, and it will reward you in the long run.

As a business owner, you simply have to believe that you are going to need to pay well for performance. If someone performs, you have to go out of your way to make sure they are incentivized to continue to perform. I strongly believe in large performance bonuses. The dollar amount has to be big enough to move the needle.

I know this goes against the grain—most of my peers increase profits by decreasing salaries or by letting high-paid, experienced employees walk in order to replace them with lower-paid ones. My company has been successful because I do the opposite: I strive to increase my wage expense for my top performers.

Pigs get fat. Hogs get slaughtered. Do not get greedy. Share with your team.

Redeployment

When someone consistently underperforms, you have to take swift and decisive action. Redeploy them in a position that will be a better fit, or remove them.

A weak performer disrupts the performance of others. If someone keeps failing at their job, it can cause the whole engine to fail.

People carry baggage around with them. Sometimes, to deal with their own baggage, they try to put it on the shoulders of those around them. You know the type: they had a bad moment in their personal life, so they bring it into the workplace and take it out on everyone around them, making everyone miserable.

When someone consistently brings the drama of their personal life into your business, get rid of them. Do not allow toxicity to hang around.

Does that sound harsh? You bet. I struggled for a *long* time with letting anyone go. I'm an optimist! I always see the good in everyone. I was the leader who would say, "You can be great at anything."

I had a hard time firing anyone, because I didn't want to hurt them.

But then I realized that by *not* firing that toxic person, or that person who underperformed without fail, or that person who made everyone else miserable, I was choosing to actively hurt all the other employees. I was choosing the problematic employee over everyone else.

That made firing people a lot easier.

MANAGEMENT

You mobilized your team (systems) and gave marching orders (processes), and you have your fuel (your employees). Now you need people in place to help you ensure that the vehicle runs the way it's designed to.

Managers are the people you put in charge of execution. They are the ones who should be checking the oil, refueling the gas tank, and taking care of scheduled maintenance.

Managers are completely different from entrepreneurs. At the start of your side hustle, you're going to be both. But as you scale, it becomes harder and harder to do both well. For me—and I think this is true for many side hustlers and entrepreneurs—management strategy and techniques were never personal strengths (although I studied them). I was too nice for the managerial role.

Managers are execution specialists. To execute, you must be both loved and feared. I preferred to be loved. In management you must be both loved and feared, and if you have to choose just one? Well, Machiavelli taught us that fear lasts far longer.

Your managers are quite simply the check-and-balance enforcers of your company. They are there to hold people accountable. With consequences.

Here are the characteristics you should look for in your managers.

Leaders

I believe that nobody is born a leader. People must be transformed into leaders. Self-confidence is the single most important characteristic needed, but with humility; leaders must be secure enough in themselves to expose their own vulnerability and tap into the spirits of their teammates to extract the best performances possible.

A self-confident leader lifts people up and is not threatened by the success of others. A good leader leads by example and will be on the front lines of a battle—and be willing to fall on their sword.

Look for a leader who has empathy. That empathy will allow them to be confident and decisive.

Coaches

Managers also must be great coaches, able to teach each employee what to do and how to do it better next time.

A great coach is able to evaluate the strengths and weaknesses of each player. In part, this helps the coach understand what goals are achievable. Setting goals that are too easy doesn't motivate anyone; setting goals that are unrealistic and out of reach is downright demoralizing. A coach needs to hit that sweet spot in the middle that pushes players without breaking them.

Think about what happens in the gym. If your trainer wanted you to increase your reps or the weight you lift by 12 percent, you could probably manage that—and then compound that growth over time. But if your trainer tried to double your bench press in a day, you wouldn't even try.

Slow and steady growth, with realistic goals set by an insightful coach, also compounds over time. By the way, this is another area where my natural optimism sometimes isn't helpful. I struggle over exercising restraint in planning out goals—I think my business can accomplish anything. It's important that I have competent managers in place who can, like great coaches, add a dose of reality.

Ability to Execute

Your managers have to be able to walk the walk as well as they talk the talk. Execution is a critical component for the successful manager. Execution includes:

- **Motivation:** The manager has to find a way to get employees to begin and continue executing the play.
- **Evaluation:** The manager has to assess performance constantly.
- **Adjustments:** The manager has to decide what to do about under-performance—whether to reallocate talent or pivot on strategy.

There are shelves of books written about each of these aspects—and entire graduate schools of business devoted to studying management and training better managers. So I'm not even beginning to scratch the surface of all there is to know about management.

The main takeaway for you at this stage of scaling your side hustle is that *the best manager for your business may very well not be you.*

PRACTICE TIP

Organizational Chart and Workflow Chart

The previous chapter ("Mobilize") was about assembling your troops. This chapter ("Marching Orders") is about giving direction to your troops. Helpful tools for visualizing the mobilization of your troops and giving them direction are an organizational chart and a workflow chart.

> Systems and processes are like yin and yang, or sun and moon; they are two separate things, but intertwined. You can't make one without considering the other.

Sometimes you get lost and you need a map for direction. The organizational chart and workflow chart will show you who and where your teammates are on the map. People are still the most important part of both your systems (mobilizing) and processes (marching). Sometimes you need to know where they are to give the right direction.

Step 1 (System): Create Your Organizational Chart

If you have a small business, you should create an organizational chart, which itemizes positions and duties. A good org chart will illustrate a chain of command. Think of your org chart as being like the rules of a board game. Everyone must know the rules to play.

Chain of Command

The org chart should show who reports to whom. If you have a side hustle or small business, your org chart should be flat. It should not look like a pyramid. There should be no more than one layer of direct report between you and any employee. If there is a problem, employees should report either directly to you or to a manager who reports to you.

Duties

Side hustles and small businesses sometimes require employees to be capable of doing projects from A to Z, as there are no departments separating the assembly line. This makes capturing everything an employee does difficult. However, you should still list out anchor duties. You need to know who is responsible for which tasks so you can track and measure progress. Every duty should either support or promote the value that your customer expects.

Step 2 (Process): Draw Your Workflow Chart

Sequence of Events

After you draw your organizational chart, you should create a workflow chart. The workflow chart should chronologically map out the sequence of action items necessary to get to your output. Your output is the thing you deliver to your customer. The action items should reference who from the org chart in step one above is responsible for each duty.

Value Maintenance

Every action item along the workflow chart should either support or promote the value that your customer expects. As you create your process by breaking it up into sequenced action items, keep in mind that it is easy for a team member to forget the contribution their role provides to the end value they are delivering to the customer. It is your responsibility as a leader to remind them as motivation.

Quality Control

In addition, the action items in your workflow chart should be places where someone could come in with a checklist to audit the quality of work. If you are a side hustler scaling to a small business, you may not have the budget to hire an independent auditor. You may have to do it yourself or make all the parties on the assembly line responsible for the quality of the work being produced. A person should accept a work in progress (WIP) from the prior action item only after they confirm with a checklist that the WIP meets a reasonable standard. Please note that if you use this technique, you need to have a high level of trust in your staff and you need to control the velocity of the WIP.

Measurement

For extra credit, you can come up with some metrics to track improvement. As I grew, I stopped measuring my success by revenue. There is such a thing as bad revenue. Today, I measure the team's success by quality, as measured by customer satisfaction. I measure the client's satisfaction by reviews, and I measure employee satisfaction by constant dialogue. Find your own ways to measure your success.

CHAPTER 13 ☯ FORMATIONS

*The third step toward scaling up on the Tao of
the side hustle is to show the world your value.*

AS YOU SCALED YOUR SIDE HUSTLE IN THIS PART OF THE
book, you mobilized your troops and then you gave them marching orders.
Now it is time to position your troops in formations to show the world the
value you could provide. Some call it marketing; I like to call it educating.

Before we get into all that, want to know why I decided to scale up
to a small family business? Besides growing to achieve more free time
and financial rewards, I wanted a place to train my daughters in what I
have learned.

When done correctly, running your own business gives you back
some control over your life. I remember the days my family had to pay for
groceries with quarters we found in the house—we had no control over
our lives. We were completely dependent on our jobs to give us what we
needed. The side hustle gave me back some control.

I wanted both salary and profit for my kids. The best way for me to
do that was to walk the walk. I embodied the Tao of the side hustle.

I am in deep in this side-hustle-to-small-business game. I believe in it so much that I want my kids to have this perspective.

FAMILY COMES FIRST AND YOU COME LAST

Let me tell you my reason for growing. This process is tough, and before you start you need to be clear about your own reasons for doing this.

I loved my summers in Korea. The Korean side of my family is originally from a city called Busan at the southern tip of the Korean Peninsula.

People from Busan are very proud because during the Korean War in the 1950s the North pushed the Southern forces all the way south to Busan. But Busan would not fall. If Busan had fallen, the only place to go would have been the water. The people of Busan dug in deep and held their ground.

Slowly, they pushed back.

Something cool about Koreans is that they say their last name first and first name last (the Chinese do the same). My mom's family name is Kim. She once told me that if we were in Korea, she would have named me Kim Hyun-In.

Last name first, first name last. Your family first, then you.

I wanted to build something bigger than myself as an individual. I decided to continue to grow my business because I wanted a place for my family to develop, fall back on, and grow in the future. I wanted to put my family first and myself last. It is a mentality, a lifestyle. I want my future generations to have a place to develop.

Wealth and power come and go. Your kids can lose everything from a random event. Don't believe me? Ask the Romans, the czar of Russia, the dinosaurs, or the rulers of any empire that collapsed throughout history. This is why adaptability is the most important character trait.

Your job as a parent is not to give your children a fancy house or a big inheritance. Get that out of your head. That comes and goes.

Your job as a parent is to make your kids good people and prepare them for the future. Just as martial arts teaches character traits like discipline, respect, and hard work, entrepreneurship through side hustles teaches adaptability, time management, and financial responsibility.

Whether you are asking your kids to run a lemonade stand, detassel corn, cut grass, or develop an app, get them out there trying.

Your business can become that incubator for future generations. It can be your legacy. A side hustle is a great place for any family to start. Do not look at your side hustle in terms of years. Look at it in terms of generations, and it will change the way you measure growth.

When you started your side hustle, most likely you were using your friends and family as a starting point for customers. As you grew and stabilized your business, you probably expanded to everyone within your sphere. Now what? How do you attract people who may have never heard of you?

As your company grows, you will need a more systematic and scientific approach to generating new business and more revenue. At the same time, you will want to retain all that has brought you success so far.

Why did your sphere of influence help you in the beginning? Trust. Your first customers trusted you, or they took a chance and learned to trust you in their first interaction.

> In the end, trust is the only sustainable form of marketing and branding. The trick is getting people to trust you.

Now you'll have to develop a marketing and branding strategy around a story that connects with your customers, demonstrates your value, and begins to create trust.

Jin was a young warrior monk—naïve but powerful. With unmatched speed and skills, Jin was undefeated across the lands.

After a typically lopsided victory, Jin approached an old teacher, the chief elder, with a difficult question.

"Which form of martial arts is the best and most effective?" Jin asked.

The teacher smiled at the question. With a twinkle in his eye, the chief elder replied, "My young warrior, that is an excellent question. But it is like comparing the beauty of the sunrise to the magic of the sunset. The answer depends on the color your eyes wish to see that day."

This was not the answer Jin was looking for. Frustrated, he asked again, "Teacher, I understand you are trying to teach a lesson. But . . . there are clearly better and worse forms of warfare. There has to be one that is better than all the others. I want to know the answer so I can focus on that."

The old teacher replied, "Which is better: religion or science?"

"I believe in science," Jin quickly replied. "There is no proof of God."

The chief elder said, "Hmm. You might be right. The thing about religion is, it cannot prove there is a God. But the thing about science is, it cannot prove there is not a God. There is evidence on both sides. The middle ground is what we call faith."

The old teacher paused for a moment, then continued slowly. "You as a person have the gift of choice. You choose what to believe in, and what is best. There is no right or wrong answer."

Jin still did not like this answer and pressed the question. "Teacher! Respectfully, you speak of philosophy. But I am asking about real life!"

The old teacher said, "Come train with me. Let me see if I can help you."

Jin agreed. The next day, he visited the chief elder again, ready to spar. But the chief elder began to practice taijiquan (tai chi). Jin half-heartedly followed. He had never believed much in this art.

The old teacher noticed. "Did you know that the martial art taiji-quan constantly makes the moves of the yin and yang? In each one of our movements?" he asked.

"Of course," Jin replied sarcastically. "You never let me forget."

"And do you know what the yin and yang is?" asked the old man.

"The balance of opposites?" Jin replied.

"Rarely in life are there opposites," came the reply. "See the traditional yin and yang symbol in your mind. Now make two. Now flip one upside down and connect them. What mathematical symbol did you make?"

"A sideways eight?" asked Jin.

"Yes. What is that the mathematical symbol for?"

"Infinity?"

"Yes!" the old man said with a smile. "Rarely are there extreme opposites. The better view is that we are all connected, and in our lives we balance coexisting forces. Our diversity and differences only make us stronger."

The young warrior sighed. "Teacher, I respect you. But you are old, and your tai chi is not real fighting. I would destroy you in real life."

His teacher smiled. "Really? Then how about this: you and I fight, and if I win, you accept that diversity and choice only make us stronger. Deal?"

Jin laughed incredulously. "Teacher, come on. I can't fight you. You're old and gray. I'll break you in half."

"Deal or not?" the teacher replied. "Or are you scared to find out that everything you believe is wrong?"

Jin agreed. The two faced off.

Jin moved first, chasing the old teacher, whose eyes softened as he waited for the young man to get closer. Jin set up to strike. He swung with great might . . . and the old teacher stepped aside, dug his cane into the ground, then suddenly swung it upwards. A spray of dirt flew into the eyes of the young warrior.

Jin was blinded. The old teacher then stomped on Jin's foot with his cane and bumped him from behind to knock him to the ground. Before the young warrior could react, the old man had placed his cane on Jin's throat. Jin screamed in submission.

"I am surprised you yielded so quickly," said the old teacher.

"But you did not play fair!" shouted Jin. "I did not know that it was possible to use a cane in a fight that way."

The old teacher replied, "Because you couldn't see in front of you, you lost."

The yin and yang story teaches us that life is rarely strictly black-and-white; there is quite a bit of gray. Just as in the yin and yang story, in a side hustle setting, marketing, production, and distribution blend and work together in a universe that starts to feel like an infinity symbol with no real beginning or end.

Now that you're ready to bring people from far outside your sphere to your business, here's what you'll need to know.

MARKETING

Marketing is an incredibly complex and beautiful universe. However, in the end, marketing is the process of communicating your value to potential customers. The hard part is choosing the right medium to send this message. Forced content like billboards, TV commercials, and sponsored social media ads can come off as annoying if the consumer is not open to hearing the message.

You have to send a message in a way in which the customer wants to hear it. No one wants to be sold. They want you to connect with them so they have a resource when a pain point arises for which you offer a solution.

Most side hustles and small businesses do not have the budget for someone solely responsible for marketing. Typically, the owner handles most of the marketing.

When I started my side hustle, all my customers were my friends and family. As I started to grow into a small business, I needed to find people outside my friends and family.

I named this chapter "Formations" because building a community is an effective and accessible form of marketing. You can build a community by identifying an audience, educating them on your value, then demonstrating that you can deliver on that value.

Build an Audience

If you want a platform to share what you do, you should start by building an audience. Identify people who would benefit from the value you offer. Connect with them.

If you are doing it online, share your thoughts, knowledge, and expertise in videos, podcasts, or teleconferences. You have to deliver value with everything you share. There is so much content out there today. You have to focus on a target audience and really deliver a specific value to that audience.

Once you get in front of that audience, you have to stay connected to them. There are so many options for them that they can easily move on to another community.

For example, I wrote this book for people interested in becoming entrepreneurs. At a macro level, I am integrated in the business owner community; I offer members of that community practical tax, legal, and operational advice. At a micro level, I really try to connect with and get to know the people in the community.

How can you engage with a community if you are sick of being online all the time or if you just prefer to interact face-to-face? Volunteer in the community, run a marathon, or write a book. Do things you enjoy, and you will attract like-minded people. Try to genuinely connect with them on a personal level. In the end, you want to build relationships with people you enjoy being around.

Do not sell them! You need genuine connection here. The old-school hard sell is dead.

> There is a golden rule of advertising: advertise to others the way you want to be advertised to. Another way to think of this is to create a community that your customers can be a part of.

Be generous with whatever it is you are offering. You should be building friendships through trust and integrity.

Once you have the audience, educate them about what you do. Give value first before you offer any service.

Educate

I would strongly advise against just spending a bunch of money on targeted social media advertising. Today, the ad market is incredibly saturated, and it's difficult to break through the noise without a massive spend. People are busy. Do not distract them. It just makes them angry.

Instead, educate your customer. People want control. They want information so they can make informed decisions. Today's customers really educate themselves before deploying their hard-earned dollars.

The most effective advertising I've used is content. I like to educate my potential customers with free material.

I don't worry that I'm giving away secrets or that potential customers will read my advice and act on their own. Generally, customers will have done their own research anyway before they speak to you.

There are two types of knowledge, which you must really understand to know your client:

1. **Knowledge of:** These are the general rules of a subject matter. Everyone can research these online. They may even be researching on your competitors' websites.
2. **Knowledge how:** This is how to execute that knowledge to cure some pain.

For example, I may have the knowledge of heart surgery, but I would have no idea how to execute it. I need a specialist.

> You can freely share the "knowledge of."
> Your reason for existence is to provide the "knowledge how."

Customers know what their problem is, but they still don't know how to solve it. So they are looking for someone they trust to help them. Reading your high-quality, free, and easily accessible content creates the beginning of trust.

Sometimes a "do-it-yourself" customer uses what they learned to actually solve the problem on their own. That's not a loss—they were not going to be a paying customer in the end anyway. And this scenario is not that common. Most people who take the time to read your free content have a problem that will require your expertise to solve.

Demonstrate

If someone gives you the honor of an opportunity, then you need to meet the customer's expectations by delivering the value you promised.

Word-of-mouth marketing from a trusted relationship is incredibly powerful.

When you deliver on the promise and you have a happy customer, they generally share their experience. That social proof is the most powerful form of marketing.

A way to develop word-of-mouth marketing is to create a binding relationship with people by delivering value. The three parts to that delivery are perceived value, actual value, and evolving value.

Educating your audience is a way to develop perceived value. Perceived value is an opportunity for you to build a connection with someone by making them aware of the value you bring to a pain point in their life. The audience needs to make an informed decision about whether you are the right option.

If someone in the audience decides to give you an opportunity, you must deliver actual value by delivering on the promise. A dull saw that can't cut won't stay in the tool chest long. You need to deliver something of value to stay in your customer's tool chest. You had better be able to cut and stay sharp.

Trust me, your customers are seeing advertisements for other sharp saws. They need to know you are capable of delivering the value associated with meeting their need on their schedule.

I focused on making sure that my perceived value would be delivered if I was called upon—that I would deliver actual, consistent value to people. I didn't want a one-night-stand relationship; I wanted a lifelong relationship.

I believe it's better to focus first on satisfying your base of customers, and then on getting new ones. Getting new customers is far more expensive than retaining existing ones.

Whatever you did to get into your customers' toolbox, make sure that you are maintaining that.

> I never went viral. I only ever wanted to be
> useful. Viral comes and goes. Being useful
> lasts forever.

Finally, assuming I was able to deliver, I wanted to start creating evolving value. As my customers changed over time, I had to adapt and evolve to meet their needs. By putting yourself into your customers' shoes, by seeing and understanding their problems, you should be able to anticipate their evolving needs and adapt your business to address them.

For example, customers loved our all-virtual approach and remote, online solutions. But some documents (in our traditional legal world) still need a "wet" signature. So we offered two solutions: either the client could come in (which no one ever wanted to do) or we could travel to their location and offer a curbside signing for a small premium.

You need to connect to your customers to be conscious of their current needs and their needs in the near future. Talk to them and connect to them. If they love you, they may even end up becoming ambassadors.

AMBASSADORS

Some people will love you. In place of advertising, many businesses now rely on champions. Brand ambassadors, influencers, evangelists, champions—these are different names for essentially the same role. Champions use their own authentic voices to talk about your business, your products or services, and their experiences with you. That authenticity then breeds trust in potential customers.

You have to give these champions your time and attention. If someone is consistently sending you referrals, show them love.

In many sectors brand ambassadors and influencers are far more influential than any PR firm or advertising agency. The social proof they provide can connect you with new communities you might otherwise be unable to reach effectively.

The opposite of a brand ambassador is a brand assassin. Brand assassins share the frustrations of their bad customer experience online.

Customers have so much power now. Internally at my business, I tell my team that this is a buyer's market. The buyer's ability to influence other buyers' purchasing power is incredible.

You need to try to not only solve customers' problems but make them feel good about it. When everyone offers similar products and services at similar prices, it ultimately comes down to the way you make a customer feel. The customer experience reigns supreme. There are very few industries left where the product or service is so rare that the seller can be a jerk to the buyer and get away with it.

One caution: be selective with the people you partner with. Make sure you understand all the brand attributes of a potential ambassador or champion. You don't want to attach yourself to someone who will later polarize some portion of your community.

If your business continues to grow, then you may have to hire a professional dedicated to marketing. Marketing gets really complicated as you grow, but the preceding approach will be highly effective for you as you first begin to scale.

——— PRACTICE TIP ———

Stop Interrupting Your Customers and Start Connecting with Them

Forcing people to see your pop-up advertisements is *so* early 2000s. People are busier than ever and get so much thrown at them. It's no wonder that consumers get mad when you interrupt them.

So stop interrupting your customers and start connecting with them. Here is an approach:

Step 1: Show the customer your value and what makes you different. There is something special about your product or service. Something that makes you different compared to the other players in the market. Something that you are better at. If not, you might have to go back to the drawing board. Once you discover what makes you special, communicate the information with the people who would find it interesting.

Step 2: Give that information to your target audience—the consumers who find that information important. You want to make sure they have immediate access to that information at their leisure. Do not force-feed. People hate being interrupted.

Step 3: Do not sell products or services, but create experiences. If someone gives you an opportunity, give them a good experience. As you grow, you will learn the importance of social proof to your marketing strategy. Hopefully, your satisfied customers will share their experiences online so others will have social proof to rely on.

CHAPTER 14 ☯ DEPLOYMENT

*The fourth step toward scaling up on the Tao
of the side hustle is to deploy your amazing
value to your amazing customers.*

NOW THAT YOU'VE MOBILIZED YOUR PEOPLE, GIVEN THEM marching orders, and begun to build your marketing efforts, this chapter will work through distribution (deployment).

Distribution refers to delivering your product or service to the end user. You have to deliver your value in the form in which your customer wants to consume it. There is a reason McDonald's sells Happy Meals to children in those fun boxes. The Happy Meal box is a form of distribution. McDonald's is delivering those burgers and fries in a medium appealing to the children who are consuming that food.

To really get into distribution, I believe we can look for some guidance from the Japanese word *chigyo*, which means "wisdom and practice." The concept of *chigyo* basically means that one gains wisdom *through* practice.

Understanding consumer behavior is an important part of finding the right medium of distribution. The only way to really understand your customer is by getting to know your customer through *chigyo*.

You have to know where your customers came from, where they are now, and where they are going.

In ancient Korea, there was a great white tiger who lived in a magic waterfall. The white tiger was an oracle, a gatekeeper for ancestors, and the aggregate of all the ancestors' lives and knowledge. Or so people said.

Great kings visited the tiger for advice. And the advice was amazing, for the tiger really could predict the future. Yet the white tiger showed himself only when he wanted to be seen and kept hidden when he did not.

Once a great king of Korea died suddenly, leaving his teenaged son in charge of the lands. The boy, named Victor Hyun, decided to visit the white tiger and seek the oracle's advice.

The tiger pitied the boy for his loss. So the tiger decided to show himself and appeared from behind the splashing waterfall.

"Victor Hyun, you are now the leader of all these lands. How will you rule?" the white tiger asked.

"Oh, great tiger. I have come to seek your advice. My father brought me here once when I was a young boy. My father was not the best teacher, and I have no idea what I am doing," Victor Hyun replied.

The white tiger looked perplexed. He licked the refreshing pool of water at the base of the waterfall, then paced around Victor Hyun. "Ah, yes—I remember your father, and the day he brought you here. You sound as if you resent your father. Why?" he asked.

"My father was never there for me," Victor Hyun said. "And when he was there, he was not a nice person."

"Is it a father's duty to be nice? I thought a parent's duty was to prepare his children for the world."

Victor replied, "Yes. But he was never there."

The white tiger frowned. "Was he not the leader of all the lands? That is a big responsibility," he said.

Victor Hyun replied, "He never spoke! He never explained anything to me!"

The tiger replied, "None of us are perfect. We walk around with flaws and do the best we know how to do. You must come to terms with this, and you must stop blaming your father for your own shortcomings. Reconcile with your past if you intend to have a future. A tree's branches cannot grow if the tree's roots are rotten."

Victor Hyun was intrigued by this. "I understand," he said. "Because my father was tough on me, he prepared me for this role." Then he asked the tiger, "Can you tell me how to lead these lands? The people call you an oracle of great power."

The white tiger chuckled and walked past the boy to the pool of water. "The magic is right here," he said.

The path toward the pool of water was surrounded by deep mud. Victor Hyun rushed to the pool, catching up with the tiger. "It's magic water?"

The white tiger slapped Victor Hyun in the back of the head. "No, you fool. Look behind you."

Behind Victor Hyun were his own footprints, but there was something special next to them: two additional sets of footprints, hardened in the mud. One set of an adult and one set of a young boy.

The tiger said, "I like to keep the footprints of all of those who visit me. Yes, I remember when your father brought you to me as a young boy. Those are the footprints of you and your father. He asked me to look after you."

Victor Hyun dropped to his knees and immediately began to cry.

The white tiger said, "We may not always agree with our parents, but you must always know where you come from. You must start by knowing yourself, inside and out. Life is a journey, but you cannot reach your destination without understanding your starting point. Along the way you will discover your strengths, weaknesses, opportunities, and threats. You will make the right decisions in the future when you have fully reflected on your past."

Victor Hyun smiled and felt a great release in his chest. The white tiger noticed the burden lifting from the boy. "Forgiveness and reconciliation feel good, don't they?"

Victor Hyun said, "I forgive you, Father. Thank you for the lessons." And the boy stood, looked at the tiger, and said, "I know now who I am and what I must do."

But the tiger was gone. Only the splashing of the waterfall remained, along with the peace in the boy's heart. He walked away from the pool of water, stepping in the footprints made by his father years ago. He would go on to be the greatest ruler he could be.

We must take lessons from the past to build our future. The son and the father are really the same, or at least an extension of each other.

Lessons from the past will illustrate a path to the future in the context of distribution as well. Distribution strategies are centered around human consumption (i.e., we want distribution to be built around the way we consume). For example, consider lunchtime eating in the downtown area of major cities. Traditionally, restaurants and vendors were built around offices with workers. During their lunch break employees would head out to grab food and eat at a restaurant. Today, many companies offer the option to work from home or follow a hybrid model. If you are working from home, you probably do not have the same need to go downtown to grab lunch. These restaurants now need to adjust their strategies.

Distribution strategies vary based on the type of business you are in. For example, business-to-consumer distribution is very different from business-to-business distribution.

A good starting point for side hustlers in businesses of all sorts is to ask these three fundamental questions:

- What business are you really in?
- How does your customer want to consume what you offer now?
- Where will relevant consumer behavior evolve to in the future?

The answers will give you some guidance on ways to deliver your final product to the consumer.

WHAT BUSINESS ARE YOU REALLY IN?

Consider this threshold question: What value are you giving to your customer? The answer will affect how you distribute that value.

For example, before the development of streaming, the video store was the distribution model for movies. After features ran in theaters, movie studios distributed videos to customers through video stories like Blockbuster (and before Blockbuster became the biggest player, there were thousands of small, independent video stores).

For the store owners, it wasn't the best business model—they had tons of overhead and no control over product.

The store owners misunderstood what business they were in. They thought they were in the DVD rental business. But actually, they were in the content business. The DVD was just the method of distribution.

When Netflix came along, it offered an alternative: instead of having to go to the video store to look for DVDs, you could get the DVDs delivered to your home, through the mail. This took a huge bite out of the brick-and-mortar video store business.

Eventually Netflix mastered streaming, and this became the dominant form of distribution. The new mode of distribution of content replaced—no, destroyed—the old mode. Netflix had to wait until the mass consumer market's infrastructure (that is, smart televisions and high-speed internet) caught up before the streaming could take off.

The customers were tired of traveling to the video store, tired of returning the rentals, and tired of getting charged late fees if they did not do it on time.

Ask yourself: What is the core value I am providing?

Once you know the answer to this, you should next turn your attention to your delivery.

HOW DOES YOUR CUSTOMER WANT TO CONSUME THAT VALUE NOW?

As our society evolves, consumer behavior evolves. The way we consume as a society is so different from that of prior generations.

Currently, if you have a business-to-consumer side hustle, you will most likely need to focus on easy, fast, and frictionless delivery to your end customer. The customer wants to save time and energy. If you have a business-to-business side hustle, you will most likely need to focus on supply chain management.

Your supply chain is the flow of goods or services that are needed to create your end product. For example, most car companies do not manufacture the stereos (or most other parts) that go into their cars; they buy the stereos and install them. Those car stereos and other car parts are all part of an automaker's supply chain.

But what about the components that go into each stereo? Often the stereo maker will also rely on various manufacturers to supply the individual components, which it will then assemble into stereos.

So the automaker's supply chain includes not just the direct suppliers, but the suppliers to the suppliers. And so on.

If you are part of a supply chain stream, you must focus on seamless integration with the upstream and downstream players in your chain. Most buyers are less concerned with pricing (at least in the beginning of the relationship) than with your ability to deliver without disruption.

There's another layer here. There may be a chain reaction if anything goes wrong. For example, if another component's design creates a vibration that impedes the use of the stereo, all the players in the stream—the car dealers, the automaker, the other suppliers, and you—will be involved in finding a solution. The actual damages and consequential damages associated with something like this could be massive. Make sure your contracts include some sort of liquidated damage clause limiting your risk exposure to lawsuits.

HOW WILL CONSUMER BEHAVIOR EVOLVE?

Society is evolving at an incredible velocity. We are currently in the technological revolution. However, there are subcategories to this revolution.

When computers were first introduced, they merely helped process data. However, as computers evolved, they helped connect humans.

The first generation of the web (Web 1.0) allowed creators to post content to consume. The second generation (Web 2.0) introduced a more social aspect, where content creators and web users could interact.

The third generation (Web 3.0), which we are beginning to see, proposes some pretty drastic changes. If these changes occur, they may involve significant evolution of our consumer behaviors.

Web 3.0 sounds like something out of a futuristic sci-fi movie—a virtual world where users can interact with each other on the web as if they were interacting in person.

Two technologies critical to Web 3.0 are blockchain and artificial intelligence.

I believe these technologies will disrupt traditional distribution in interesting ways in the coming years.

Blockchain, a digital general ledger distributed across a network of computers, is the underlying technology behind cryptocurrency, but it has a wide range of applications. As a giant digital ledger, blockchain is really a form of accounting. It enables "smart contracts," self-executing contracts with the agreement built into the code.

Think of a soda vending machine. You put in quarters and push a button, and a can of soda comes out. Blockchain and smart contracts operate in the same way: participants along the supply chain can create a code for a smart contract wherein certain events occur that trigger the creation of something else. A supply chain transaction that traditionally required a person or a business to move something down the stream may, in the future, happen without that intervention. This may have drastic, streamlining consequences for all kinds of supply chains.

Artificial intelligence—essentially, machines that have learned to think—will surely have a big impact on our future. Again, the likely result will be to streamline processes and remove human intervention. Forecasting is an obvious candidate. Already AI forecasts my potential purchasing desires and decisions. In the future, AI will probably forecast supply levels and coordinate distribution of services—tasks human beings do today.

It's also likely that blockchain and AI will begin to cross-pollinate and find their own uses, beyond what humans are envisioning today.

These are some pretty intense concepts. You may not know all the answers, but you may want to think about the ways you can evolve your side hustle to find its place in Web 3.0 with blockchain and artificial intelligence. I believe the future holds incredible opportunities for side hustlers who are adaptable to change. I believe Web 3.0 will be the era of the side hustler.

─────────── **PRACTICE TIP** ───────────

Know Your History to See Your Future

Throughout this chapter we discussed how your past shapes your future. This is an important lesson in life, but it is especially important in distribution.

I see a huge opportunity for side hustlers in the world of distribution. Distribution is closely tied to consumer behavior. This chapter illustrates the velocity of our behavior changes.

Look at my side hustle. My differentiation was that I would do house calls. I would go to the client. I succeeded because I changed an option for distribution.

As we evolve, our appetites and consumption patterns change. Side hustlers are close to the customer, so they can be the first to forecast and react to these changes.

Look across the board at newer technology such as food delivery applications, ride shares, and online retail shopping. The online experience has changed distribution by making consumption easier.

Take a step back and see if you can make it easier for your customer to consume your value. Here is an approach:

Step 1: Become a student of your industry. Find your core value and go back and study the evolution of that value relative to the customer it has served. For example, let's look back at eating at restaurants. Eating out at restaurants is almost three thousand years old. People need to eat, and restaurants have taken on the responsibility of preparing meals. Some restaurants are suitable for social experiences such as dates or get-togethers. Some restaurants prepare convenient food for workers. However, the core value of these restaurants is serving food. The other stuff is just supportive or a differentiation.

Step 2: Determine how you are delivering the value today. As we evolved, our core need to eat remained the same, but the distribution of meals changed dramatically. We still have restaurants, but we also have food delivery applications on our smartphones, which allow us to have restaurant food delivered to our homes. We have food preparation companies that make healthier alternatives to eating out. To throw a major curve ball into the mix, remote work has been adopted by many companies. This has completely changed many people's eating patterns: remote workers do not need restaurants for convenience anymore, as they can eat at home.

Step 3: Project how you would deliver that value in the future. What will your business look like two, five, and seven years from now? If you can nail this step down, you might get your next side hustle idea. Will convenient healthy eating take greater market share for those on the move? Will artificial intelligence signal us when we should order takeout from our favorite restaurants? Will science offer us synthetic food alternatives? These are questions to ponder. It is my belief that demand for the core value of eating in a social setting will continue. However, the way we experience this may change.

The preceding approach gives us food for thought.

Distribution is a great place for side hustlers to focus on differentiation. There is a ton of opportunity here today, and there will be more opportunity tomorrow.

CHAPTER 15 ☯ PEACE

*The fifth step toward scaling up on the Tao of the
side hustle is to stop working and get out there and
live. There is more to life than business and money.*

YOUR SIDE HUSTLE DOES NOT DEFINE YOU. IT IS A VEHICLE
created for the purpose of getting you from salary to profit. That's it. If it
does not work out, try again and again until you get it right.

If it does work out, at a certain point you will have to say "enough."
When you are stable and comfortable, you will want to turn your attention to happiness and making the world a better place.

After my small business started to grow and eventually stabilized, I
gained more and more time.

I had the time to recover from my Achilles tear. Tai chi taught me
how to train every day even when I was hurt. After I recovered, I continued to train every day, and after three years of training, I am back in the
saddle with my original side hustle.

This year I was invited back to film another project for a big studio.

My original side hustle has returned to my life. I am no longer the crazy twentysomething, willing-to-do-anything side hustler. I am now a fortysomething father of two with a full-time law practice, but I've managed to achieve a balance: I can still practice martial arts for some of the biggest action franchises in the industry. It makes me happy, and in the end, that is the reason we took this Tao of the side hustle. The Tao is all about a path to balance.

Profit is only part of your business. It is a really important part, especially at the beginning. However, I really do believe each business is a live organism, existing in an ecosystem we are obligated to maintain. We are not robots. Although efficiency and effectiveness are important, they are not the goal. Profit is not the goal; the promotion of humanity is the goal.

If you measure yourself and your success by the amount of money in your bank account, you have missed the point of life. Measure yourself instead by how you have made the world a better place, by how you have touched lives, and by what you have accomplished.

Get out there and help people in need. Touch lives and change the world.

Money is merely a medium of exchange (which may be about to undergo some massive changes), created by governments. Yes, it's also a tool for living, especially for those without it; the cost of a sandwich is very important to a starving person. But at a certain point in a successful career, too many sandwiches will rot in your picnic basket.

In other words, you must balance your business with life.

There was once a young monk named Qigu and an old monk named Ming. Qigu had recently transferred to the Buddhist meditation school run by Ming. When Qigu arrived, he was bullied by some of the other students at the school.

There was one bully in particular named Dasheng. Dasheng was several years older than Qigu, was much bigger than the other kids, and had a lot of friends.

Qigu went to see Ming for advice.

Qigu said, "Monk Ming, I do not want to be a tattletale here, but there are these students who are really making my life miserable. Especially Dasheng. What should I do?"

Ming said, "Ahhh, bullies. Some children are especially cruel. Since ancient times there have been those who prey upon the weaknesses of others. Their actions are merely a reflection of their own insecurities. The greatest power you can have over someone is to refuse to let their words hurt you."

Qigu said, "Well, thank you for that, Monk Ming. That is really interesting, see, but the thing is . . . yeah, they use mean words all right, but they also punch and kick me too. The mean words, those are pretty brutal, but it is the hitting that I am struggling to get over."

This really caught Monk Ming's attention. He said, "Oh dear, that is terrible. Hmm. Maybe you can reason with them? Yes, reason with them. Tell them that they need to respect you and that their actions are just a reflection of their own insecurities."

Qigu said, "Uh, well, are you sure? I feel like that won't work."

Monk Ming put his arm around Qigu and said, "Give it a shot." The two parted ways.

Qigu approached Dasheng and said, "Look, I need you to respect my feelings. I know that you are just projecting your insecurities and pain onto me. I need you to stop . . ."

Qigu was knocked unconscious.

Qigu returned to the elder the next day with two black eyes and said, "Yeah, uh, that did not work."

Monk Ming was perplexed. He said, "My brother Monk Bianjie runs a martial arts school across the way. Maybe you can meet him to see if he can provide some guidance."

Qigu went to see Monk Bianjie and said, "My name is Qigu, and I am a student of Monk Ming. I am having trouble with bullies and he said I should come see you."

Monk Bianjie said, "Bullies, huh?"

Qigu said, "Yeah. Monk Ming said I needed to talk to them and tell them to stop and respect me and that their actions are just a reflection of their insecurities."

Monk Bianjie began laughing hysterically and said, "What? That is the craziest thing I have ever heard. The only way to deal with bullies is respect. You have to get them to respect you."

Qigu asked, "Well, how do I do that?"

Monk Bianjie stood up, made a knife hand with his hand, and said, "You ever see us chop through wood or bricks?"

Qigu nodded.

Monk Bianjie, chopping through a brick, said, "Well, it's because this part of your body is very hard."

Qigu was clearly impressed.

Monk Bianjie said, "Stand up and put your hands together like this in a prayer position. Whatever you do, keep your hands together."

Monk Bianjie began blitzing Qigu with a barrage of punches and kicks. Qigu, taken aback by the power of these punches, fell backward. Surprisingly, Qigu opened his eyes to discover that he was unharmed.

Monk Bianjie said, "You see how your hands are protecting your chin, neck, heart, kidneys, liver, and other vital organs?"

Monk Bianjie pulled Qigu up and said, "When you put your hands together in a prayer position, it is a sign of self-respect, not submission. Respect starts with self-respect. If people see that you respect yourself, they know that you will not tolerate bullying. You have to respect yourself enough to stand up for yourself. I will teach you."

Monk Bianjie trained Qigu for months in martial arts. Slowly and painfully, Qigu became stronger and stronger.

During Qigu's training, Monk Bianjie told him, "In Chinese martial arts, we have a special word: *wú chǐ dàchóng*. This means "toothless tiger." Most bullies are just toothless tigers. They look scary, but they have no bite. You just need to know how to stand your ground."

After several months, Qigu returned to the meditation school, and upon his return he was greeted by his bully Dasheng.

Dasheng gathered his friends around and said, "That kung fu stuff doesn't work on me, boy."

Dasheng beat up Qigu, but this time it was different. Qigu stood his ground and fought back, and although he did not win the fight, Dasheng did not walk away unscathed. Even with the help of several friends, the bully barely won. In addition, Qigu continued to attend martial arts training with Monk Bianjie.

Dasheng continued to bully Qigu for a short time. Each time they fought, Qigu grew stronger and stronger, until he too became a fierce fighter.

One day Dasheng approached Qigu to fight, but this time Qigu smiled with an extreme level of confidence. Dasheng stopped. Dasheng gripped his stomach in pain and remembered a punch he'd taken from Qigu in their prior fight.

Dasheng turned to everyone and said, "No, let's move on to someone else."

Qigu was never bullied by Dasheng again and turned his attention to meditation.

I got beaten up so badly in my life that there came a point when I just said "enough" and drew a line in the sand. I set my boundaries. I then used side hustles to fight back. The side hustle will not come without adversity. Side hustling is a contact sport and you may take some hits, but if you keep moving forward, you will grow tougher and stronger as you survive each punch.

In the end, you have to learn how to say "enough." I am an authentic example of someone who built a side hustle into a small business. I was in a horrible place and I used side hustles to get me out. I have shown you how to use the weapons I used. At a certain point, you must learn to put the sword down and pass it to someone else.

How do you go about thinking less about money and more about the important things in life? What are the components of happiness? Here are the lessons that I have found useful in my own journey.

BE A GOOD PERSON

At some point, you will be faced with adversity. It's not a matter of if; it's a matter of when. And that's when the world will discover the type of leader you are.

Early in my career, I had a traumatic experience involving a respected leader. At one of my first jobs, at a large prestigious company, my boss was in charge of the entire division. He was impressive on the outside—smart, funny, charismatic, handsome—everything I thought I wanted to be.

Turns out he was not such a great guy. He used his power to have an affair with his secretary. As the details were about to come out, he fired her. He denied the allegations. But they were true, and he too was fired. Settlements and nondisclosure agreements followed.

His behavior was reprehensible. Rather than step up and take responsibility, he took the coward's way out. He lied, and brought down others.

Watching someone I thought was a great man and a great leader fall from grace was traumatic for me. But I learned a great deal from the experience—mostly, about what not to do.

Accountability

When you make a mistake, own it. Everyone is human. Everyone makes mistakes. Most systems are built around the idea that humans always *do* make mistakes. For the most part, people understand this and are forgiving.

Owning your mistakes can be humbling. But it preserves your integrity. It preserves the credibility of your word. And it allows all parties to turn their attention to damage control.

When things go wrong, people want to identify the problem, find the issue that caused the problem, and solve the problem. By owning your mistake, you allow everyone around you to save mental calories on steps one and two and to laser-focus on solving the problem.

My old boss made a mistake by trying to cover up a problem. As rumors began to spread, he asked his closest allies to defend his character.

Then when hard evidence came out, his allies scattered and felt betrayed by his lies. Everyone turned on him, in large part because he failed to own his mistake and hold himself accountable.

Consequences

Owning the mistake is not the end of it. There must be consequences.

When my system creates a process error or my team makes a performance error, I try my best to make restitution to the harmed party. Often this is in the form of a refund or compensation, as I want my customers to see me and my business as fair and willing to square up no matter what. If you own your mistake and show that you are trying to make amends, most people are quick to forgive.

My old boss could have come clean and owned his mistake. There may have been severe consequences—he might have lost his job anyway—but over time people might have forgiven him. Instead, he ruined the life of his secretary and permanently alienated his friends. By not simply owning his error, he compounded the consequences.

Growth

After you own your mistake and accept your consequences, you must find a way to grow from the crisis.

We are all human and will continue to make errors. But we can also use our past errors to improve. Generally, I can learn something important about either myself or my process and make a change to prevent the mistake from happening again.

BE SOCIALLY RESPONSIBLE

To put it bluntly, you have a responsibility to your community—a social responsibility to do good and have a positive impact on the people around you.

Engage with Your Community

Businesses are components of a broader community, and you must engage with and understand your community. You should hire from the community and give back to it. Businesses exist not only to produce profit but also to benefit the broader community.

There may come a time when you and your business need the support of your community. If you have not been there for your community, do not expect it to be there for you.

There are a lot of problems in the world and in your community. Some require solutions far beyond any individual person or any one business. But some problems can be at least partially addressed through the collective action of small businesses, via their actions or their combined purchasing power.

Build your business *and* influence the businesses around you. Pull the other businesses in your community toward your point of view. Stop supporting or supplying businesses that don't share your sense of social responsibility. If a company refuses to develop diversity leadership, stop buying from it. Speak to that company with your dollars.

The market may help correct abuses. But today's environment has given everyone a microphone, and with so many people speaking, it is easy for individual voices to be drowned out. If a company is truly behaving poorly, you must model for the market how that company should be treated.

No, you cannot change the world overnight. But little by little, you can make a difference.

Give Back and Create Opportunities

When you first started your side hustle, didn't someone give you a break? A first chance, a first sale, a helping hand to open a door for you? Those opportunities were like oxygen, allowing your new company to breathe. Now you must provide that same oxygen to others.

Life has not always been easy for me. I am sure you have your own struggles. I am a half-Korean, half-Polish kid from a lower-middle-class single-parent household on the Northwest Side of Chicago. My name literally translates to "wise sausage," which is hilarious when you think about it. You can imagine my childhood. I was fortunate to have the Catholic Church, the Chicago public school system, and martial arts to give me the base, community, and skills needed to grow.

As my business became successful, I moved back to my old neighborhood and started hiring people from there. There is a lot of turbulence and hate here. There have been two murders by shooting and several drive-by shootings one block from my house in just the past year.

I can leave at any time, but I choose to stay. I am from Chicago; I am stubborn and resilient. Problems motivate me to find solutions. (*That* is the Chicago way.)

Show your fellow humans kindness and forgiveness, and provide people with opportunities to build. It is good business. Do not forget to forgive.

> **Do not look for people to build things for you. Build things for people.**

As you grow, you will evolve from a scrappy underdog to a mature industry player. Young, talented entrepreneurs will seek you out, asking for a chance.

Helping young talent is not only good karma but good business. Inevitably you will find great new talent this way. You may launch the career of someone who will boomerang back to help you and your business—and maybe even work for you or partner with you. I am constantly hunting for the next superstar.

——————— **PRACTICE TIP** ———————

Charitable Giving

Want to know what you never see following a hearse in a funeral? A bank vault filled with money. You cannot take the money with you. Give it to people or organizations that need it.

Remember those old-school video game arcades with the scores on top of the cabinets? Some of those games had a limit on the high score. The number might have been crazy, but at some point there was a limit.

Visualize the number you are trying to reach. Hit that number. Then stop for goodness' sake and help others. Besides providing amazing tax benefits, giving is one of the most fulfilling things you will do in your life.

- **Business:** Charitable giving is good business. Go make money, take care of your family and coworkers, then give back. Rinse and repeat, over and over again.

  People want to see that you are part of the social fabric of the community. By giving to local charities, you are showing your support. I think the new consumer is going to demand this in our near future.

- **Personal:** Get out there and volunteer. You may not have money to give, but I bet you can make time to give. Not only does volunteering soothe the soul, but you meet and build relationships with other giving, successful people. It will be a great opportunity for you to build up your network.

There are many other ways you can give to charity. However you do it, become the engine of kindness.

CONCLUSION

I WROTE THIS BOOK FOR ALL THE UNDERDOGS OUT THERE.
The truth is, I do not have natural gifts. I never got good grades. I am short. I did not come from money.

What did I have? I tried to be nice to everybody I met, and I had the discipline to work at breaking free every single day. Then, once I broke free, I turned my attention to helping others do the same.

The most recent person I've guided—I hope—is you. I hope this book has provided you with both the ideas and the motivation to break free. Most of all, I hope this book has shown you completely new ways to think about and solve the problems in front of you.

I want to have a final moment of vulnerability here. I was in a pretty horrible place. I was beyond broke. I was so broke I could not even declare bankruptcy. My personal life was in shambles and I was trying to find a job in the 2008 market. I disclosed some things earlier in this book that I am not that proud of. I showed this part of me to illustrate to people that there is no shame in hitting rock bottom.

In fact, hitting rock bottom is quite liberating. I gained something incredible by hitting rock bottom. I gained a sense of freedom, because I stopped caring about the way others thought about me. You cannot make everyone happy. So stop trying.

You need to stop caring about the perfect picture and get rid of all the cropping, filters, and touch-ups. You need to look at yourself for all the good and the bad. Appreciate the beauty of poorly timed, untouched pictures with crooked smiles, blemishes, and all the other flaws.

These were the photos taken of you as a kid when you did not care about the way people looked at you. This was the time when you had the most imagination and took the greatest risks. You let it all go.

This is not my story. It's yours. This is the part of the movie when you're down, but some guide—some North Star—picks you up and helps you move in a new direction.

I hope this book sends good vibes throughout the universe and world. I wrote this book because I genuinely believe that anyone can develop a successful side hustle, and I wanted to show you how.

Here is my call to action to all my fellow side hustlers and underdogs. If you were in a rough place and you found a rope that you were able to climb, then help others. Share your story and inspire others. If you see others starting a side hustle, do not stand idly by. Help them, support them, and get them going. Give them opportunities to grow.

This is our Tao. This is our path to balance. Let us start walking.

ACKNOWLEDGMENTS

I WOULD LIKE TO THANK MY WIFE, EMILY HOLMES, AND MY daughters, Ellie Kai and Victoria Hyun. Thank you to my parents for making me who I am. Next, I would like to thank my literary agents/ attorneys Tim Brandhorst and Marc Lane. You two are truly amazing. Thank you to Matt Holt for giving me the opportunity. I would like to specifically thank Jamie and Jon Cesaretti for all the guidance.

I would also like to thank the Chicago public school system and the Catholic school system for giving me a community when I was lost.

I would like to thank both the Shaolin Temple in Dengfeng, China, and Wudang Mountain in Shiyan, China, for inviting me to train and teaching me so much.

ABOUT THE AUTHOR

Photo by Brian McConkey

DONALD HYUN KIOLBASSA, JD, CPA, is a licensed Illinois attorney and certified public accountant. He is the managing partner of Donald Hyun Kiolbassa, Attorney at Law Ltd., where he focuses on property law, estate planning, and corporate law. As a licensed attorney and CPA, he has helped thousands of clients over the past sixteen years. Prior to becoming an attorney, he worked at KPMG LLP. When Donald is not practicing law, he is an avid martial artist. He is the motion capture martial artist behind some of the biggest video game action franchises in the industry.

IT'S TIME TO HUSTLE

Keep up the momentum on your journey to personal accomplishment and prosperity.

Find inspirational and practical resources for your side hustle.

Watch videos of Don and see stories from the book come alive in animation.

Connect with Don to share your progress and success.

Visit TaoOfTheSideHustle.com